THE NAET CLINIC OF OTTAWA
536-A DOVERCOURT AVE. OTTAWA, K2A 0T9
(613) 728-2579   www.naetottawa.com

A Guide for Caring Teachers and Parents

THE IMPOSSIBLE CHILD

in school — at home

Doris J. Rapp, M.D., F.A.A.A., F.A.A.P.
Clinical Assistant Professor of Pediatrics
State University of New York at Buffalo

Introduction by Lendon Smith, M.D.

Copyright © 1986, 1989
by the Practical Allergy Research Foundation.
All rights reserved.
No part of this book may be reproduced in any form or
by any electronic or mechanical means, including
information storage and retrieval systems, without permission
in writing from the publisher, except by a reviewer who may
quote brief passages in a review.

Published in the United States of America by
Practical Allergy Research Foundation
P.O. Box 60, Buffalo, N.Y. 14223-0060

Library of Congress Catalog Card No. 86-60049
ISBN 0-9616318-1-3

DEDICATION

This book is dedicated to Joseph E. Miller, M.D. (Mobile, Alabama) for sharing his extensive knowledge with many physicians. Because of his instruction and example, many doctors are now able to help children and adults who would have been erroneously labelled functionally or emotionally ill. His expertise has enabled us to pinpoint the exact cause of many previously elusive complaints, and to help patients in a manner that was not previously possible.

It is also dedicated to the many other doctors who, since the turn of the century, have published articles and books to help enlighten the public and the medical profession. They have helped to increase the public awareness of the multiple and varied aspects of illness related to foods and the environment. The following list represents some of the major doctors who have had the moral fiber, courage and compassion to come "out of the closet." Each of the following has withstood peer pressure and unjust criticism to help those in need. Each of these doctors has made their patients, his prime priority.

Theron Randolph, M.D.	*William Rea, M.D.*	*Marshall Mandell, M.D.*
Francis Hare, M.D.	*Dan R. O'Banion, Ph.D.*	*Phyllis Saifer, M.D.*
Albert Rowe, M.D.	*David King, Ph.D.*	*Gary Oberg, M.D.*
Herbert Rinkle, M.D.	*John MacLennan, M.D.*	*Richard Mackarness, M.D.*
Arthur Coca, M.D.	*William Crook, M.D.*	*Jonathan Brostoff, M.D.*
Frederick Speer, M.D.	*John Crayton, M.D.*	*Jean Monro, M.D.*
Benjamin Feingold, M.D.	*Lendon Smith, M.D.*	*Ronald Finn, M.D.*
Iris R. Bell, M.D., Ph.D.	*James O'Shea, M.D.*	*Alan Franklin, M.D.*
Joseph McGovern, M.D.	*Allan Lieberman, M.D.*	*Vickey Rippere, Ph.D.*
Alan Levin, M.D.	*Michael Schachter, M.D.*	*Joseph Egger, M.D.*
John Gerrard, M.D.	*William Philpott, M.D.*	*Jonathan Soothill, M.D.*
Sherry Rogers, M.D.	*Ted Kniker, M.D.*	*S. Lingam, M.D.*
Francis Waickman, M.D.	*Lawrence Dickey, M.D.*	*Alexander Schauss, Ph.D.*
Richard Mabray, M.D.	*George Kroker, M.D.*	*Sidney Baker, M.D.*
David Morris, M.D.	*Marvin Boris, M.D.*	*Michael Radcliffe, M.D.*

ACKNOWLEDGMENTS

Nancy Dlugokinski: for her most capable supervision of the updated revision of this book.

Barbara Rellinger, R.N.: for her artistic design of our logo and her continued aid with medical references and resource material.

Pat Jagodzinski: for her organized and efficient assistance in many, many ways.

Norah Foley: for her continued perseverance and patience in computerizing the necessary information to create the updated revised edition of this book.

Ruth Schultz: whose sincere genuine interest in artwork and layout added another dimension to this book.

Gloria Siblo: for her many generous contributions in both time and energy. Her editorial expertise, innovative suggestions, and practical advice have greatly enhanced the quality and applicability of this book.

Jan Telban, R.N., Joan Lalime, R.N., Sandy Brzezinski, R.N., and Helen Goeltzenleuchter, L.P.N.: for helping to monitor and collect accurate objective documentation of the many surprising changes which occurred so often in some children during allergy testing.

Rozalind Adams, Mary Lang, and Mary Jarosik: for special assistance.

Nancy MacDonald: for her creative illustrations.

Paula Burk, Ph.D., Louise Giuliano and George Kunz: for reading the original manuscript.

Arlene Mazikowski and Cindy Rose: for their extensive typing of the updated bibliography.

Dorothy L. Bamberg, R.N., Ed.D.: special thanks and gratitude.

TABLE OF CONTENTS

PART I

RECOGNIZING BEHAVIORAL REACTIONS
TO FOODS OR OTHER FACTORS . . 1

PART II
COMMON CAUSES
OF BEHAVIORAL SYMPTOMS
AND POOR SCHOOL PERFORMANCE . 23

PART V

SUMMARY 85

PREFACE

The prime concern of dedicated educators and caring parents is to provide quality education for children. Teachers and parents, however, are faced with youngsters who perplex and confuse them. There is a subset of children who appear to learn well and easily on one day, but not on another. They seem unable to function consistently well in school. They often act appropriately but suddenly, for no apparent reason, their behavior can exasperate the most patient teacher or parent. Other children appear unable to learn or behave most of the time. Some are too active; others are too tired and fatigued. Many have recurrent headaches, legaches, or digestive complaints.

This book explains how a teacher or parent can detect which youngsters might have an unusual, unsuspected or unrecognized adverse reaction to foods, chemical odors or common allergenic substances, i.e., dust, molds, pollens and pets.

The material in this book will provide information to help verify suspicions, and suggest what can be done after possible cause and effect relationships have been observed. By recognizing the latter, children may be able to realize their full learning potential, and their present and future quality of life may be enhanced.

Many references are enumerated throughout the text. The exact sources of information are provided in the appendices. These may be useful to parents, educators, physicians, psychologists, probation officers, social workers, counselors, and others interested in specific learning or medical problems. This list is designed to provide more in-depth discussion and explanation for the public. Scientific references are listed for those who desire more specific, objective, controlled or blinded data.

This book discusses only **one** aspect of behavior and learning problems in children, namely, the possible role of foods, chemicals and common allergens. Many children have other or additional causes for the same problems. The children's physicians, and specialists such as neurologists, psychologists or psychiatrists, and endocrinologists, in particular, may be needed to more fully elucidate the specific causes of some youngsters' problems. Parents should check with their child's physician before trying the suggestions discussed in this book.

INTRODUCTION

I have long been a fan of Doris Rapp. She dared to say that children and adults can become "different" when they eat or breathe allergenic material. She then went on to document with videotapes and movies what she had noticed, and after years of trying to get the public's attention she has come out with this significant book. If they will read it, it will show the skeptics that the brain is connected to the body. The brain cannot produce gas or a rash when it is stressed; it only shows changes in thought, perception and behavior. If any of these three things are altered, teachers, parents and peers will notice the child is "different."

Many standard doctors are laboring under the limited view that we were trained to believe in medical school: If someone has odd or non-compliant behavior and there is no obvious disease by examination or laboratory test, that person should be sent to the psychiatrist. It is thought that some distorted parent-child relationship is producing the inappropriate response. If a child wet the bed, it meant that he hated his mother. If he had a headache, he had sublimated aggression. If a child was hyperactive, he was basically depressed. And if he grew up to be a criminal or psychopath, he had incorrectly internalized his parents' teachings of right and wrong.

Now because of the work of Doris Rapp we can sometimes blame foods and things we inhale. Mother is off the hook. She thought she was doing her children a favor by making them drink a quart of milk every day. Sometimes she just made them sensitive to the stuff. Dairy products can make some people become hyperactive, some hypoactive, some get mean, some turn blue with asthma, others develop a headache, and a few become depressed, too tired, or wet the bed.

We probably all need to see a psychiatrist every now and then to get some help sorting out our lives and goals. But we must remember and hope the psychiatrists have learned that sometimes inappropriate activity and behavior can be physiological and not psychiatric.

Even the American College of Allergists made this statement a few years ago: "Allergies do not do everything, but they can do anything." After reading this book, and nodding assent page after page, I would like to propose a new "Rappism:" If someone — or anyone — is behaving rationally or appropriately for the situation, and then for no good or valid reason becomes depressed, aggressive, uncoordinated, somnolent, stupid, pale, silly, spacey, that is, "different," one must search for foods, dust, molds, pollens or chemicals which might have been eaten or inhaled during the previous 1 to 12 hours.

We have learned over the years that when youngsters "acted up," it meant that they had not been properly disciplined as children, and needed to be "taught a lesson." That may be true, but current evidence suggests that some people are overly sensitive to their environment. My experience is that the hyperactive children who are allergic, often are ticklish and have a fair complexion. They notice everything and must respond to the stimulus. Telling them to "Stop it!" is like telling the ocean to stop roaring. If children only hear negatives while they are growing up, they are more likely to develop a poor self-image. I was not surprised to learn from teachers that there was one hyperactive child in every class in 1950; now five or six are disruptive, inattentive and easily distracted. After Halloween and Easter it is the whole class! It is known that 75% of prisoners in our jails today were hyperactive children; 75% of them were battered. I think I know why some of them were battered. They were rude, mouthy, did not mind and could not sleep.

Teachers, counselors, probation officers, parents, grandparents, doctors and anyone who has a friend, lover or relative must know about the facts in this revealing book.

Lendon Smith, M.D.

PART I

RECOGNIZING BEHAVIORAL REACTIONS
TO FOODS OR OTHER FACTORS

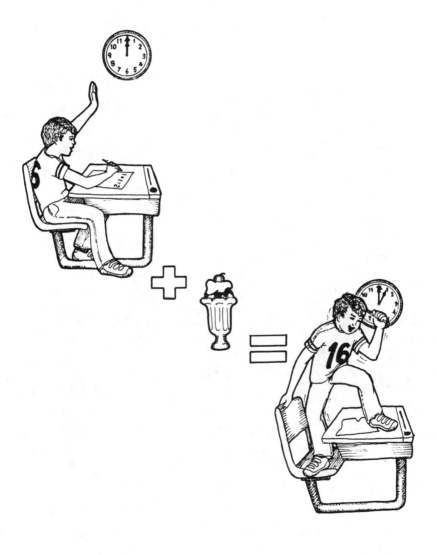

CHAPTER 1

SIGNS OF BEHAVIORAL REACTIONS
(# *1-5, 7-12, 15, 21, 26, 42, 44-49, 57-67, 85*)*

There are innumerable reasons why some children, occasionally or frequently, appear to be unable to learn or suddenly act inappropriately in class. Sometimes these changes can be related directly to foods which have been eaten, or exposure to chemical odors or common allergenic substances.

For reasons no one has explained, fair-haired, blue-eyed boys in particular, appear to have an increased propensity for behavior and activity problems. Be assured, however, that any child or adult can manifest the identical changes enumerated below because of unusual reactions to various things in our environment.

Facial Or Body Clues

There are a number of typical facial, or body clues which may indicate that a youngster might be having an adverse reaction to inhaled or ingested items. It is not unusual to notice that some "problem" youngsters suddenly develop *glassy* or *glazed eyes* along with:

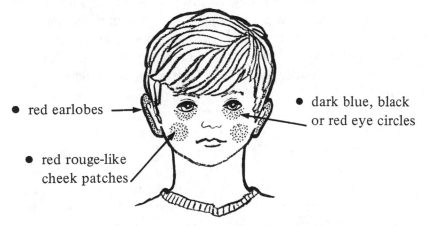

● red earlobes

● dark blue, black or red eye circles

● red rouge-like cheek patches

*Throughout this book, the numbers that follow this symbol, #, indicate the references in the Bibliography in Appendix F, page 115.

Other physical characteristics that also may be seen in children who experience such changes in activity or behavior might include:

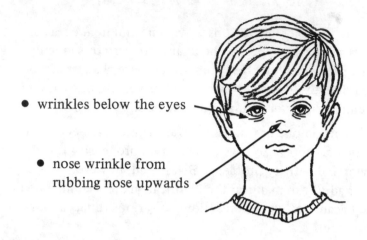

- wrinkles below the eyes

- nose wrinkle from rubbing nose upwards

The children who manifest these characteristics often act as if they were *"spaced out,"* and reprimands may not seem to be acknowledged or heard. Some act *sleepy* or *tired,* others are *fidgety* and *cannot sit still.* Not uncommonly, some appear to have frequent *lapses in their concentration.* They *cannot stay focused* on their reading material, or seem unable to respond normally to advice or directions. These types of *inattentive* behavioral patterns may be noted, in particular, after the ingestion of common offending foods such as artificially colored sweet beverages or cereal, candy, popcorn or corn products, chocolate, peanut butter, tomato products (pizza), milk or dairy products, baked goods which contain additives or preservatives and apple, grape or orange juice. These foods, as well as many others, can cause **some** children to develop symptoms of *hyperactivity, depression, fatigue, headache, abdominal discomfort, asthma* or *hayfever.* Teaching can be a disappointment and challenge for educators when such symptoms exist. Parents can be perplexed, disturbed and distraught by their child's erratic, intermittent inability to learn and behave.

Complaints commonly associated with adverse reactions to foods, chemicals or common allergens also include (*#1, 3, 46*):

- stuffiness or sniffling (*#2, 3, 46*)
- clucking throat sounds or throat clearing (*#2, 46*)
- coughing or wheezing (*#2, 71-73*)
- itchy or watery eyes
- swollen eyelids
- puffy bags below eyes
- swollen cracked lips
- itchy skin rashes, especially in the arm or leg creases
- frequent hearing loss secondary to recurrent ear infections (*#74, 75, 104*)
- sudden ear pain or ringing in the ears (*#74, 75*)
- recurrent headaches (*#1, 3, 76-79*)
- recurrent legaches or muscleaches (*#3*)
- wiggling legs, hands or arms
- recurrent intestinal symptoms characterized by nausea, bloating, pain, belching, halitosis, rectal gas, diarrhea or constipation (*#1, 3, 46, 80*)
- excessive thirst (*#1*)
- recurrent infections or absenteeism due to "not feeling well"
- unexplained facial pallor
- extreme ticklishness (*#26, 27, 103*)

Some affected children will suddenly *wet their pants,* or *soil their underwear* in response to the ingestion of certain offending foods. Milk, fruit or fruit juice, or raisins commonly cause bed-wetting or bowel problems. Some children wet at night because of dust or mold allergies.

The ingestion of milk and dairy products appears to be associated with one or more of the following complaints: clucking sounds, throat clearing, nasal congestion, legaches, halitosis, constipation, diarrhea, bed-wetting or recurrent ear infections.

Activity Or Behavioral Clues

(#1-5, 7-12, 15, 21, 25, 42, 44-49, 57-67, 86, 94-97)

The activity or personality changes often seen in affected children may include:

- overactivity*, loudness, silliness, irritability, aggression, vulgarity, depression (*#1, 83*), or hostility (*#44, 45, 94-97*)

- fatigue (*#1, 85*), falling asleep after eating or persistent yawning

- inability to sit still*, concentrate or think

- easy distractibility*, and impulsiveness*

- crawling under furniture or in dark corners, refusal to be touched or to respond normally to simple directions (*#95*)

Changes in writing and drawing (*#21, 95-97*)

Changes in activity and behavior are often associated with differences in children's handwriting or drawings. For example, a youngster suddenly may write illegibly, large or unusually tiny, backwards, in mirror image form (writing with reversals), or upside down. Sometimes they write from the right to left side of the paper. Writing frequently reflects children's activity levels. The writing of *hyperactive* children may become so large that they are unable to write on an ordinary-sized piece of paper. *Depressed* and *withdrawn* children may make a dot for their name, write in a constricted manner, or refuse to write anything.

Some children manifest *depression* or write suicidal notes, for example, after eating certain foods or after exposures to pollens, molds, dust or chemical odors. Other children may develop asthma, hayfever, cry easily or crouch in a remote area due to these same items. The responses are specific and individualized in each child (or adult).

---

*These are characteristic of the attention deficit disorder (A.D.D.).

This six year old girl was obviously depressed when exposed to molds or damp weather. She expressed her feelings in her writing and her behavior. She became depressed, withdrawn, angry, and untouchable. When she was allergy skin tested for a mold sensitivity, she manifested this identical type of behavior.

Illustration 1
A SAMPLE OF A NOTE WRITTEN BY THIS 6 YEAR OLD ON A DAMP DAY

Typical note after play outside on a rainy day. It says: "Who likes me because I am almost all the time stupid!"

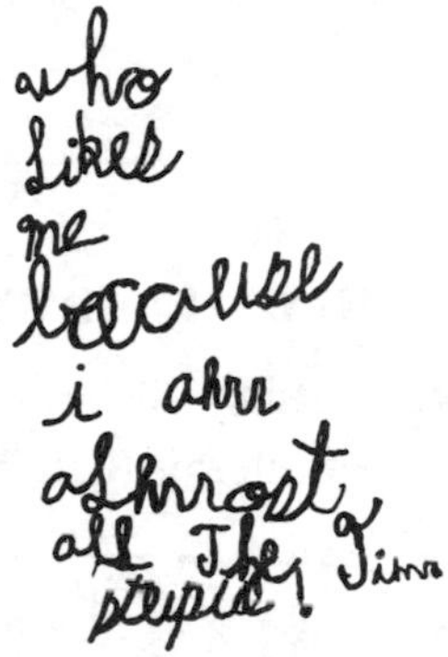

The following note was written by the same girl shortly after appropriate treatment with her mold allergy extract. It clearly illustrates a change in attitude and mood. She has changed from cursive writing to bold printing.

"I guess everyone likes me anyway! Love, Sarah to everyone."

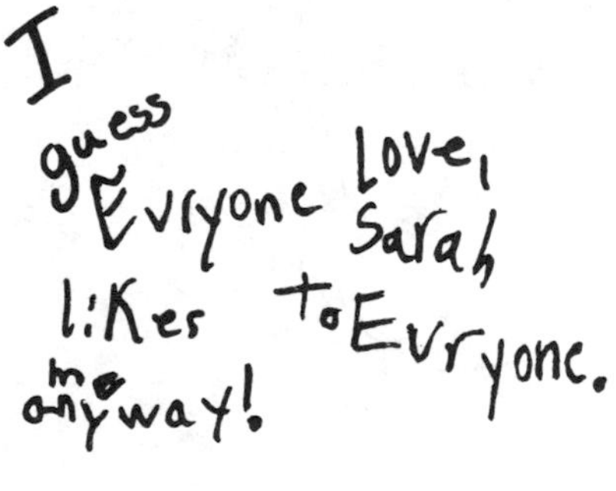

Other students may draw knives or blood, which indicate *violence, aggression, anger or hostility* (*#44, 45, 94-97*). Some reactions can be caused by an ingredient in a candy bar or exposure to some seemingly innocuous odor such as the smell of molds, freshly-made popcorn, or chemically-treated paper. Responses to offending substances are highly individualized.

A number of three part drawing and handwriting samples are illustrated in the rest of this Chapter. These refer to the period:

- **before** a child is skin tested with an allergenic substance
- **during** the reaction from an allergy skin test or food
- **after** the reaction has subsided because of allergy treatment

Illustration 2

TEST WITH MOLD ALLERGY EXTRACT

The FIRST DRAWING of this 6 year old girl illustrates her positive attitude before an allergy test for a mold.

Baseline drawing.

This SECOND DRAWING, made shortly after a mold allergy skin test, illustrates a kick. At that time, she screamed if anyone touched or went near her. She was angry and very upset. She covered her eyes with her hair and folded her arms defiantly over her chest.

Drawing during reaction to a mold allergy skin test.

This THIRD DRAWING was made after she had been treated for her mold sensitivity. At that time, she was smiling, affection-ate and crawled on her mother's lap to kiss her. Her illustration reflects this change in attitude.

Drawing after treatment for a mold.

Other youngsters may write a *vulgar* note using socially offensive words because of the way a food, odor, or air pollutant affects them.

Illustration 3

TEST WITH SCHOOL AIR ALLERGY EXTRACT
11 Year Old Boy

Drawing Before Test	Writing During Test	Drawing After School Air Treatment
KOI	ŠUCKS Royal	SWORD tail
• Pleasant and cooperative	• Vulgar, overactive and aggressive	• Pleasant and cooperative

Illustrations 2 and 3 are documented by movies or videotapes which clearly demonstrate that at the same time there is a change in handwriting or thought content, there may be an accompanying behavioral change. (*#95, Part 3*)

Sudden *aggression* or *hostility* can be manifested in the form of *pinching, pushing, biting, spitting, kicking or hitting.* The children may attack an object such as a toy, book or desk. At other times they may hurt a younger child, their teacher, mother or even themselves.

Some children seem to have an inordinate propensity to bite and chew. They *bite* anything or anybody. This biting tendency is particularly evident in children aged two to four years. The biting stage is often replaced with *hitting* as these children grow older.

Changes in school performance
(*#1, 3-5, 8-12, 15, 46, 48, 50, 57-67, 95-97*)

Some youngsters may find they are inexplicably *unable* to *read* or *do arithmetic* at certain times. One specific subject in their school work may be affected while others are not. Grades may vary from A's to D's before and after lunch in the same subject. A child may have a passing mark on one day and fail on the next day.

Occasionally I.Q.'s of children change in conjunction with an improvement in their activity and behavior. This four year old youngster was remarkably better after six months of treatment. After diet and environmental changes, combined with allergy extract therapy, he no longer spat, bit, hit, jumped, and threw his toys. He could concentrate easily and play calmly for hours.

Illustration 4

AN INTELLECTUAL SUMMARY
EVALUATION OF A CHILD
(Wechsler Preschool and Primary Scale of Intelligence — WPPSI)

Scale	Oct. 1984 Age 4 yrs. Scaled Score	Interpretation	April 1985 Age 5 yrs. Scaled Score	Interpretation
Verbal I.Q.	81	Low Avg.	109	Avg.-Above Avg.
Performance I.Q.	99	Avg.	110	Avg.-Above Avg.
Full Scale I.Q.	88	Low Avg.	110	Avg.-Above Avg.
Behavioral Observations:	Hyperactivity Short Attention Span Impulsive		Rare Tantrums Long Attention Span (hrs.) Excellent Reading Scores	
Interventions:	Physical Therapy Speech/Language Therapy		Physical Therapy Speech/Language Therapy and **COMPREHENSIVE ALLERGY TREATMENT**	

12

This series of pictures and handwriting demonstrates how this same five year old can regress in a few minutes after an allergy skin test for wheat, in contrast to a placebo or mock skin test. When he ate a slice of wheat bread, the same changes occurred in his behavior, actions, writing and drawing within 22 minutes.

Illustration 5

TEST WITH WHEAT ALLERGY EXTRACT
Drawings and Handwriting Changes In 5½ Year Old Robert

Before Testing	After Placebo Skin Test	After Wheat Allergy Test

Drawing

Writing

• Normal actions and play	• Normal actions and play	• Spitting, biting throwing, jumping, and uncooperative

A videotape of the above allergy tests vividly demonstrates these changes (*#96*). The implications of these documented changes in Robert are serious and extremely significant. Children who have this type of sensitivity at a young age could be placed inappropriately in a class for retarded or learning disabled children. The results of I.Q. or psychological testing could vary greatly depending upon what some children eat or smell prior to or during such evaluations. Everyone must be alert to detect why some children appear to learn and act much better at certain times. The answer may be surprisingly simple as soon as the teacher or parents look for cause and effect relationships. Unusual responses to environmental factors always should be seriously considered as a possible factor in handicapped children who appear to require special placement in the school setting. Part of the handicap in some children could be an unrecognized, unusual response to an allergenic substance.

Changes in speech

Speech problems in some children can be related to specific exposures (*#3, 21*). They can suddenly *stutter, use very rapid* or *high pitched speech,* begin to speak unclearly, lapse into *baby talk,* or appear unable to form sentences. Sometimes they *bark,* make *chicken sounds,* start to *giggle* inappropriately, make strange *gulping* or *throat clearing* sounds, or other annoying *vocal noises* which interfere with routine classwork (see pages 68-70, patient report).

Changes in coordination

Fine motor coordination, manifested in the way a pencil is held or how children are writing, can be affected. Some children suddenly will write with the *"other"* hand.

Alterations in *gross motor coordination* may be evidenced in the child who breaks the pencil on the desk or rips the paper while trying to write with extreme vigor. Others may manifest a change in stride, the way a door is closed, or inordinate *clumsiness.* Sometimes their inability to judge distance when *running* can cause repetitive body bruises or injury as they bounce or bang their way across a room and into a wall. Others appear to respond slowly to directions in the classroom, as well as in gym class. It is not unusual for some children to manifest repetitive *facial twitches* or annoying *leg wiggling* in the classroom. Rarely, even epilepsy has been proven to be precipitated by foods (*#87, 88*).

Changes in attitude

The behavior of some pupils may become irrational, inexplicable and impossible (#3, 85). Such students suddenly *disrupt* an entire class by their *outbursts* and *inability to sit* or remain quiet.

Changes in senses

An abnormal or increased *sensitivity to sound* (# 74), *light* (#91), *or touch* is evident in some affected children. At times these youngsters *cover their eyes or ears* with their hands in an attempt to shut out light or sound. Such action can be caused, at times, by exposures to something to which they are sensitive or allergic.

Others may suddenly *dislike being touched* by anyone and visibly recoil, even from loved ones (#95). Some children may **never** have tolerated cuddling from infancy through early or late childhood. Other children might suddenly *remove all or part of their clothing* because they dislike contact with anything, or because they suddenly feel too hot. The latter behavior is most common in, but not confined to, preschool-aged children.

Occasionally, a child will hear well at one time, and poorly at other times (#74, 75). This is commonly due to recurrent serous otitis, or fluid formation, behind the ear drums. There are several causes for this type of problem. Most children are helped by conservative otologic care, and others require some form of surgery. In some children, however, the problem persists because it is due to an unsuspected allergy. Milk, in particular, can cause this problem during infancy. Other foods, chemicals such as natural gas, dust, pollens or molds are thought by some physicians to contribute to this malady in some toddlers and older children. A combination of changing a child's diet, making a home more allergy-free, or treating a child with an allergy extract can relieve ear problems in select children. The children who are helped by these measures often have allergic relatives plus one or more of the following: dark eye circles, nose rubbing or wiggling, sneezing, sniffling, stuffiness or nosebleeds. They may disrupt the classroom with their annoying clucking or throat clearing sounds.

Illustration 6

The following is characteristic of the type of audiogram seen in some allergic children. It shows a low tone conductive hearing loss. There is a characteristic gap between the air conduction (O-X) line and the upper line which represents bone conduction (<>).

TYPICAL ABNORMAL PURE TONE AUDIOGRAM

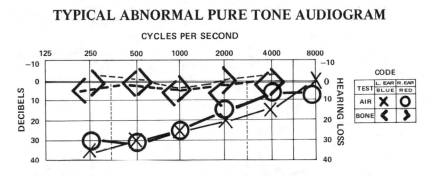

If a child responds favorably to allergy care, the air and bone conduction lines are superimposed upon one another and the hearing thresholds are within the normal range.

TYPICAL NORMAL PURE TONE AUDIOGRAM

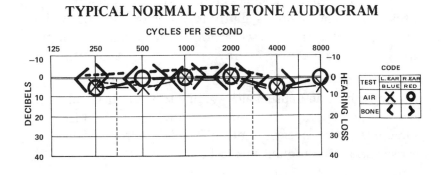

16

Some schools use tympanometry to help evaluate ear function. This electronically measures not only the elasticity of the ear drums, but also the pressure behind the ear drums (impedance).

Illustration 7

TYMPANOMETRY
PRESSURE CURVE

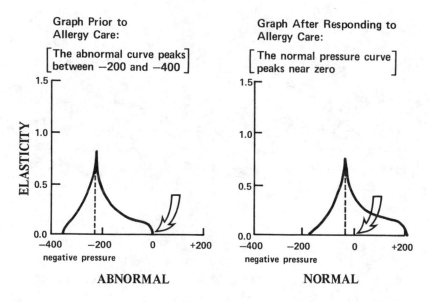

Graph Prior to
Allergy Care:

[The abnormal curve peaks
between −200 and −400]

Graph After Responding to
Allergy Care:

[The normal pressure curve
peaks near zero]

ABNORMAL

NORMAL

A positive response to allergy care is obvious within a few weeks if the allergic nose symptoms and repeated ear infections subside. Graphic proof, however, on the audiogram or tympanogram may not reflect the improvement for several months.

We must wonder how many children with a persistent hearing loss could have an unusual allergy, or a food or chemical sensitivity. Could appropriate allergy care obviate the need for surgery to insert tubes in some children's ear drums? Some ear specialists have found this to be true (*#74, 104*).

Other observable clues

An unusual persistent *body* or *hair odor* also can create a social problem. At times youngsters who are exposed to something to which they are sensitive, suddenly develop a strong, pungent odor *at the same time* that they act inappropriately. Either eating a problem food, or allergy testing a patient for an offending food or pollen can cause this same embarrassing odor in certain sensitive patients. Unfortunately, research funds have not been available to determine what is being excreted in the perspiration at the time of such reactions.

Sometimes a chronic yeast infection can cause a constant *skin odor* or *rash* which is not relieved by bathing (*#52,53*). These problems can seem worse after "sugary, yeasty or moldy" foods are eaten. Look for a white coated tongue.

A problem, which is infrequently discussed but distressingly evident, is *recurrent touching of the genitals.* This problem is often attributed to tight pants, synthetic underwear, colored toilet paper, pinworms or masturbation. Sometimes, however, in very young children, genital rubbing may be a manifestation of an unsuspected and untreated chronic yeast or mold sensitivity. This condition may have been caused by a previous excessive need for antibiotics, or the use of birth control pills in older girls. Some physicians have found that appropriate yeast medication combined with allergy extract treatment for yeast (candida), and a yeast free diet, sometimes can resolve this problem easily and quickly (*#52, 53, 101*).

~ Remember ~

If the cause of a child's inability to learn or behave is evident on a **daily** basis, children often manifest any of the previously mentioned changes **every day**. If the learning problems are only evidenced in school, some contact or exposure that occurs *only within the school environment* may be the cause. It is not unusual for similar unacceptable activity and behavior problems also to occur at home **if** the **same** offending or allergenic factors are evident in **both** the school and home environments.

18

Changes in writing and drawing during allergy skin testing

Educators and parents should try to relate sudden changes in a child's ability to write or draw to what the child ate, smelled or breathed prior to the change. The following illustrate the types of changes that can occur after allergy testing for pollen, dust, an extract of school air, and a number of foods. The children and parents are usually unaware of the item being tested.

The children are asked to write or draw a picture before testing is begun. A tiny droplet of an allergy extract is placed in the child's arm. If the child changes physically or emotionally, the child is asked to write or draw again. Then the child is treated with the correct dilution of the *same* allergy extract which caused the reaction. After the child's affect and personality have returned to normal because of this treatment, the child is asked to write and draw again (Chapter VIII, pages 76, 79, 80).

Illustration 8

TEST WITH GRASS ALLERGY EXTRACT
Handwriting Changes In 5 Year Old Laura

Before Test   During Test   After Grass
                                          Treatment

This unusual reaction occurred during allergy testing for grass.* How would Laura write and perform during examinations which happened to be scheduled during the grass pollen season in June? Could her writing change if she had recess or gym on a freshly cut lawn?

*See Pollen Calendar, page 111.

Teachers and parents often can correlate behavior changes with alterations in a child's handwriting. The challenge is to determine why this happens in a certain place, at a particular time.

Illustration 9

TEST WITH EGG ALLERGY EXTRACT
Handwriting Changes In 4 Year Old Joel

Before Test	During Test	After Egg Treatment

- Normal activity
- Very red earlobes, hyperactive
- Normal activity

Joel wrote larger, upside down, and backwards during the allergy skin test for egg. His writing returned to normal after treatment with the correct dose of a standard egg allergy extract.

Would he write abnormally in school after a typical breakfast of egg?

Teachers and parents should try to determine **why** a particular child suddenly writes backwards.

Illustration 10

TEST WITH SCHOOL AIR ALLERGY EXTRACT (#95-97)
Handwriting Changes In 9 Year Old Edward

Before Test	During Test	After School Air Treatment

• Normal	• Withdrawn, throwing toys, headache, red ears, earache	• Ears less red, headache and earache gone, behavior appropriate

Because of unacceptable behavior noted mainly while he was in school, an allergy extract was prepared from the air in Edward's school. He frequently would crawl under the desks, become withdrawn, speak in a vulgar manner, twitch, bark, become aggressive and develop a headache. Repeatedly, when he was tested with the special allergy extract prepared from the school air, he acted in the same manner as he did in school. Although his reactions were videotaped, the type of scientific analysis required to determine the specific factor in the school air which caused this child's unusual reaction has not been undertaken because of a need for research funds.

Other children have become very tired, irritable, depressed or complained of being unable to think clearly when they attended certain schools.

Illustration 11

TEST WITH MILK ALLERGY EXTRACT
Changes In Drawing Of A 3 Year Old Boy

Before Test	During Test	After Milk Treatment

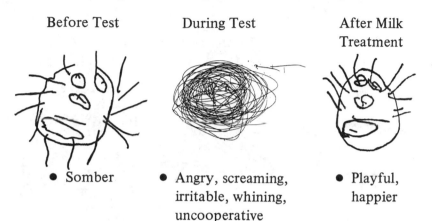

• Somber	• Angry, screaming, irritable, whining, uncooperative	• Playful, happier

Could this child learn if he had milk for breakfast or lunch?

Illustration 12

TEST WITH MITE (HOUSE DUST) ALLERGY EXTRACT
Handwriting Changes In 8 Year Old Don

Before Test	During Test	After Mite (Dust) Treatment

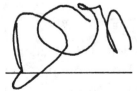

• Quiet and calm	• Rocking in seat, kicking on floor, earlobes red	• Quiet and calm

Would it be a surprise if a dusty auditorium, library or play room caused his behavior to change?

Illustration 13

TEST WITH CORN ALLERGY EXTRACT
Drawing Changes In 11 Year Old Jill

Before Test	During Test	After Corn Treatment

- Normal activity
- Giddy, made chicken sounds, and acted inappropriately
- Normal affect and personality

Have you ever seen inexplicable deterioration of a child's actions or drawings in a classroom or at home?

~ Remember ~

The practical application of Illustrations 1-13 is that changes, similar to those which occur during testing for single allergenic substances, also occur when a problem food is eaten or a child is exposed to common offending allergens. Newer methods for diagnosis and treatment with allergy extract sometimes can relieve these types of responses (Chapter VIII, pages 75-82). In addition some of the obvious long term effects of intolerable action and behavior probably can be ameliorated or prevented (*#2, 3, 46, 47*).

PART II

COMMON CAUSES
OF BEHAVIORAL SYMPTOMS
AND POOR SCHOOL PERFORMANCE

~ Remember ~

If teachers or parents have noticed that the types of changes which have been described alter some children's ability to learn, the following may provide clues to explain *why* this happens.

In general, the causes may be found:

- **INSIDE THE SCHOOL**
- **OUTSIDE THE SCHOOL**
- **AFTER EATING A FOOD**
- **AFTER SMELLING A CHEMICAL ODOR**

CHAPTER II

CAUSES OF SYMPTOMS INSIDE A SCHOOL

(*#2, 3, 33-43, 46*)

At times, the cause of learning problems is related to the odors from materials that are present in many schools or homes. These include cleaning materials, synthetic carpets, soft vinyl plastic items, wall paneling which emits formaldehyde, re-modeling or reconstruction materials or the odor of various types of insulation or pesticides.

Other common offending odors include the smell or scent of perfume, aftershave, hairspray, aerosols, facial tissues, fabric softeners, chlorine, mothballs, new polyester clothing or tobacco.

A number of frequent odors inside schools are related to certain classrooms or activities. These include the smell of chemistry labs, industrial arts supplies, printing or photographic equipment or swimming pool chemicals. The moldy odor in lavatories, shower areas, gyms, locker rooms, or near swimming pools also can cause symptoms. Mold-sensitive children may become ill in basements which have been previously flooded or in other areas of the school which happen to be damp. Some children can be affected by natural gas leaks from stoves, or the aromas of food in a cafeteria or in cooking classes. The odor of popcorn, for example, could permeate a hallway so that a youngster in a nearby classroom, who is exquisitely sensitive to corn, might begin suddenly to act in an inappropriate or unacceptable manner. The same is true if one child eats a peanut butter sandwich while sitting near a child who is extremely allergic to peanuts. The latter child can become ill with asthma, or begin to misbehave merely from breathing the odor of the peanut butter.

Other objects frequently found in classrooms or at home which could cause symptoms include odorous marking pencils, pens, crayons, putty, glue or paste, fresh newsprint, clay, Play-Doh, mimeograph or chemically-treated paper, typing correction fluid, chalk, paint, art materials, pets or pet food or holiday decorations (e.g., Christmas trees).

Studies show that some children become hyperactive if they sit directly under fluorescent lights, or if they sit in close proximity to a television set (#91). Some children will wiggle if they are seated on a hard *plastic* or a *Naugahyde* chair, but will stop wiggling and sit quietly if they are seated on *wood*.

~ Remember ~

Ordinary school or household dust is a common problem for many children who have allergies. The dust in school auditoriums or in other infrequently used rooms commonly causes classical hayfever and asthma. Dust, however, also can be an unsuspected cause of changes in the affect and behavior of some children. If a child sits near a heating duct, for example, the circulated dust and odors from gas or oil combusion could trigger typical allergic symptoms or behavior problems.

Illustration 14
EXPOSURE TO CLEANING FLUID
Handwriting Changes In 5 Year Old Boy

These numbers were written by a 5 year old boy shortly **before** an exposure to a cleaning fluid while in a medical office.

Baseline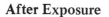

The sample below shows how he wrote within minutes **after** the odor permeated the room where he was sitting.

After Exposure

On one occasion, at 1 P.M., a bus driver, unfamiliar with this boy's sensitivities, insisted that he sit in the *back* of the school bus. He was driven about five blocks to another school. When he was taken home at 3 P.M. his mother noticed he was standing bewildered in the center of the road. He had lost his jacket, school lunch box and books. Confused after gym class that afternoon, he had put his left shoe on the right foot and the right shoe on the left foot. The boy stated he had no idea where his belongings were, his head was pounding and he felt terrible. He did not begin to act normal until 7:30 P.M. that evening.

The multiple chemical exposures which are ubiquitous in our society present a constant challenge for this child and his family. This child and parents, for example, are aware that he reacts similarly to the odor of perfume, the smell of his neighbor's lawn mower or to a few breaths of automobile exhaust. It is imperative that his teacher be aware of the role of odors in relation to this child's erratic school performance.

CHAPTER III

CAUSES OF SYMPTOMS OUTSIDE A SCHOOL

(#1, 12, 30, 37, 40-43, 46)

These commonly include the odor of:

- a school bus
- freshly cut grass or weeds
- weed killers or herbicides used on lawns
- automobile exhaust from nearby roadways
- outside factory pollution
- nearby construction odors
- freshly asphalted driveways, parking lots or streets
- municipal tree spraying programs
- aerial chemical spraying of fields

Temporal Factors Causing Sudden Symptom Flares (#2)

In particular, educators and parents should try to relate the occurrence of symptoms to a particular day, week, month or year.

For example, if some children seem to have symptoms as soon as they arrive at school, a number of factors must be considered. The cause of a child's misbehavior could be due to exposures to plastic, perfume or tobacco, chemical air pollution or exhaust fumes on the school bus. (The latter is sometimes diminished if a child sits in the *front* of the bus.) It is also possible that a child's ability to learn could be affected by what a child ate for breakfast, the type of toothpaste that was used on a particular morning, or the odor of a cosmetic which a parent or child had used in the bathroom.

Pollen Seasons (*#2*)

Most people know that pollen can cause hayfever and asthma, but some children manifest personality changes or an inability to learn, year after year, *only* during the pollen season.

Fall symptoms

If a child has symptoms only during the *first few weeks after school begins,* a sensitivity to the late summer and early fall mold spores and weed pollens could be the cause.

Youngsters who are allergic to molds and weeds may find that they cannot learn or act appropriately in the *fall* until *after* the *first frost.* Because of this, these children have a distinct disadvantage every year when school begins.

Winter symptoms

If a child has symptoms only during the *winter* or *very cold months*, the sensitivity could be related to dust, molds, pets, indoor odors or commonly eaten foods.

Dust-sensitive children suddenly develop learning problems when the heat is turned on during the late fall months because this can circulate accumulated dust through the duct work leading from the furnace to various rooms.

Some children, who have difficulty only during *winter thaws,* may be reacting to molds found on the grass after the snow melts.

Spring symptoms

If a youngster has difficulty only during the *early spring* months **when trees are budding**, one should consider tree pollen. If medical or learning problems are evident mainly on damp days when it is very rainy outside, a mold sensitivity could be present.

Spring to summer symptoms

If the symptoms in some children occur mainly during the *late spring* and *early summer* **when the grass needs to be cut,** one should consider grass pollen. If grass pollen is a problem, some youngsters routinely may do poorly in their final year-end examinations in contrast to their satisfactory performance during the rest of the year. The odor of freshly cut grass, even in the late summer or early fall, can cause allergic symptoms. An outside recess can precipitate much more than asthma or hayfever. Some children will have a total personality change affecting their ability to learn.

Illustration 15

TESTS WITH DIFFERENT ALLERGENIC ITEMS

Handwriting Changes In 6 Year Old Jason

	Writing During Baseline	During Allergy Skin Test	After Allergy Treatment
Grass			
Mold			
Rye Grain			

The handwriting samples of this six year old boy illustrate that *different* allergenic items can cause *similar* changes. Notice that with each item, Jason's handwriting returns to normal after he is tested with the correct dilution of the appropriate allergy extract. Treatment with this dilution appears to enable this child to be exposed to these allergens with fewer or no symptoms (Chapter VIII, pages 79, 80).

~ Remember ~

The exact periods for pollination vary from state to state, but
in general the weather bureau's reports for each area of the
country will note that each specific type of pollen is evident
in the air at almost the identical time, year after year. In upper
New York State, for example, tree pollen begins to affect
youngsters from late March to mid May. Grass pollen begins
to be a problem in mid April or early May, and causes symptoms until about the first week in July. Molds begin to cause
symptoms in late July, and by early August, weed pollens are
also evident. Both molds and weeds cause symptoms until the
first frost in mid to late October. In lower New York State
the pollination season would begin approximately two weeks
earlier. In other areas of the country the period of pollination
may begin earlier or later, and last for more or less time
(Pollen Calendar, Appendix E, pages 111-114).

SCHOOL RECORDS CAN PROVIDE ANSWERS

School Nurse Records

If a youngster acts inappropriately, investigation of the school nurse records might be informative. These records may reveal a definite pattern of symptoms related to a particular time of the day, week, year, or to a specific classroom, teacher or weather condition.

School nurses, also, can help some asthmatic children detect if some school exposure is causing wheezing which may or may not be associated with a change in attitude or ability to learn. Some children's doctors have prescribed simple, inexpensive plastic devices to monitor the lung capacity of asthmatic children (Appendix D, page 107). If a school nurse notices, for example, that a child blows 250 with this device prior to lunch and only 175 after lunch, the foods eaten or the exposures in the cafeteria could be factors decreasing the child's lung capacity. Similar readings, before and after specific classes or exposures in different areas of the school, could help pinpoint problem areas for some children.

Clues From Preschool Records

Preschool history records, also, may provide clues indicating which children might present a **future** behavior or learning problem. For example, some hyperactive children appear to have a history of inordinate activity *prior to* birth, when they were in the uterus. The mothers of these children can frequently, vividly remember that the fetus hiccupped much too often, or that they were "sore in the inside," or cried in pain because the unborn babies kicked so vigorously. Some women can relate the surge of unusual fetal activity to a specific food or chemical exposure.

The early history of some hyperactive children also may
indicate a number of the following complaints *prior* to the
age of two years:

- many formula changes
- prolonged colic
- unwillingness to smile
- inability to sleep well
- frequent spitting or vomiting
- reluctance to be cuddled
- profuse perspiration
- constant crying or irritability
- prolonged frequent temper tantrums
- walking before ten months
- extreme crib rocking
- traumatic head banging
- excessive drooling (body length bib)

If a youngster with a history of several of these complaints is
having difficulties in school, parents and teachers should
attempt to discover if the cause could be foods, chemicals or
a common allergen such as dust, pollens, molds or a pet. The
teachers and school nurses, in particular, should identify the
time, place, date and as many other pertinent factors as
possible. Repeated detailed records may provide clues which
would otherwise have been missed.

Clues From Teachers Or Parents

It is not uncommon for teachers or parents to notice some
nuance which indicates that a child does not act or appear
entirely normal. There may be no major disruption until the
child is denied some minor request or asked to follow some
simple direction. Then a behavioral eruption ensues. Asking a
child to put on his coat or pick up a toy can cause a sudden,
total, explosive loss of control. At this same time young
children often develop a characteristic whine or repeatedly
state the same request over and over again. This happens in

spite of whatever a parent or teacher does to comply with a child's complaint.

Teachers often spend more hours per day with children than their parents because of our "working mother society." Baby sitters often do not have the background or maturity to recognize the significance of dramatic changes in youngsters. Teachers may be the only persons who see children for a long enough period of time to fully evaluate their actions and behavior. They can best compare children of similar ages. Educators not only enable the other pupils to learn better, but they decrease their own stress load to a considerable degree by helping one challenging child in a classroom.

Some teachers will consider the role of a medical detective as one more unjustified burden to add to their already excessive number of obligations and responsibilities. Some teachers, because of personal pressures and problems, may be unable to accept any additional challenge. Without special effort on their part, however, the increased awareness provided in this book may help them resolve some children's problems. Other teachers' lives and attitudes may be such that they comfortably can accept an additional committment. An "above and beyond" effort may result in much more than a feeling of personal satisfaction. It is certainly possible not only to alter the direction of a child's education, but to change the course of a child's entire life if an unsuspected cause of a learning problem can be detected.

~ Remember ~

Try to relate the temporal or seasonal factors which have been mentioned to repeated disparities in a child's ability to think, act or behave appropriately. By doing this you may find some cause and effect relationships. These observations can lead to better understanding and **practical** answers to explain why some children, who seem capable, simply cannot consistently perform as well as they should in school.

CHAPTER IV

SYMPTOMS RELATED TO FOODS

(#1-12, 16, 21, 26, 27, 31, 46)

Detection Of Food-Related Symptoms

Many educators and parents have noticed a relationship between meals and a child's level of activity and type of behavior. Ask, in particular, the following:

- Do some children react differently after a particular meal such as a "junk food snack?" Are any children different on the days when they eat candy, cereal, pizza, ice cream, cake, cookies, peanut butter, chocolate, popcorn, or drink a colored, sweetened beverage? Which children buy junk food in school or at the nearby candy store before, during or after school?

● Some youngsters have an adverse response to "good foods" such as milk (cheese, yogurt, ice cream), bread, corn, banana, egg and peanut butter (without sugar). The fruit or juice of apples, oranges, grapes or pineapple can affect many children in an adverse manner if they are sensitive to these items.

● Which children behave differently at party time? Do birthday and the celebration foods at Halloween, Christmas, Chanukah, Valentine's Day, and Easter seem to affect a youngster's school performance?

- Teachers and parents should try to determine why a child suddenly cannot write or learn after lunch. Can the change be related to what was eaten?

Illustration 16

TEST WITH WHITEFISH ALLERGY EXTRACT

Handwriting Changes In 10 Year Old Stuart Noted *After* **Lunch.**

Prior to a lunch
of whitefish

After eating fish

After initial test
showing reaction
to whitefish allergy
extract

After treatment with
the correct dilution
of whitefish allergy
extract (Chapter VIII)

- Does any child's activity or writing change after lunch? Ask why?

- Some children swap food. Parents provide "good" lunches but some enterprising pupils trade their nutritious food, such as an apple, for junk food, such as candy. Sometimes the switch is merely a preference but sometimes the desired food points to a specific food sensitivity or unsuspected allergy.

- Some youngsters steal money to buy food. It is not unusual for children to have an **intense** craving for the foods to which they are most sensitive. These children may steal to buy chocolate, soda pop, candy, popcorn, etc. The foods they buy can indicate the specific food which is a problem.

Food-sensitive children often have abdominal complaints which can range from a slight bellyache to bloody colitis. They frequently have an abdomen which becomes distended after eating. They belch, pass gas, and complain of halitosis, nausea, diarrhea or constipation. Associated headaches, leg wiggling, legaches or other muscleaches are not uncommon. If these problems occur *only* on school days, they could be related to something eaten only in school or some other factor in the school environment. If, however, the abdominal complaints occur seven days a week, be suspicious of a food-related problem due to a frequently eaten food. It is not stress related to school if the child has abdominal pain or headaches on weekends and vacations, as well as on school days.

Other youngsters appear to have mixed messages in relation to a food such as milk. For example, some children (or adults) who dislike milk intensely, seem to crave cheese, yogurt and ice cream. They often have a total dairy sensitivity, but only recognize that milk is not well tolerated. Once **all** dairy products are *totally* eliminated from the diet, their symptoms sometimes subside completely. Milk symptoms tend to include a stuffy nose, throat clearing, clucking throat sounds, chronic cough, bed-wetting, intestinal complaints, legaches, muscleaches, ear problems, fatigue, hyperactivity or some form of misbehavior. These children frequently were infant feeding problems because of prolonged colic. This complaint is frequently related to milk in the infants' formulas. If breast-feeding mothers drink cow's milk, it passes into the breast milk and some sensitive babies become irritable. A milk sugar, or lactose intolerance, should be suspected mainly in those infants or children who develop diarrhea, gas, and bloating from dairy products. Lactase-treated milk can help this illness.

Practical Ways To Detect Food Sensitivities In School

It can be very helpful to merely observe youngsters during a school or home party. Ask all the children to write their names and draw pictures prior to the beginning of the party. About 45 minutes after the youngsters have eaten, ask them to write and draw again. If any youngster becomes unusually boisterous, active, withdrawn, hostile, aggressive or silly, suspect that the change in behavior *might be* related to a food. This may be particularly true if the youngster manifests bright red earlobes, glassy eyes or dark eye circles at the time of the personality change.

Many skeptics believe that it is the excitement of any party which causes some youngsters to misbehave. Excitement, as a variable, can be eliminated by having a similar "vegetable" party. The vegetables can be prepared in creative designs.

Most youngsters become exuberant merely because they are having a party, regardless of the type. If the writing, drawing or behavior and activity, however, of some children deteriorate markedly only during typical parties, and do not change during the vegetable parties, suspect one or more of the usual party foods.

Special Diet Information For Teachers And Parents

Single or multiple food allergy diets **should not** be prescribed by a teacher, and parents should check with their child's physician before trying any diet. Educators and parents, however, must understand the basic principles related to simple diets which help detect or pinpoint food sensitivities. Educators also should urge parents to inform them if any child is participating in any type of dietary trial. If the teachers know, they can be especially observant concerning significant changes in that youngster's ability to learn or behave at the time of the dietary investigation. Children on diagnostic food allergy diets must bring their lunch to school. If parents are unaware that their child purchased a substitute lunch, evaluation of a special diet may be impossible.

Teachers must communicate with parents, and vice versa. Teachers have an opportunity to see children for many hours on school days, and readily can notice which children do not conform to the "norm."

Parents must share their observations with teachers by informing them about their child's performance at home. Teachers and parents who communicate effectively mutually can enhance a child's ability to learn.

Types of Diets
(*#1, 16-18, 20, 21, 25, 31, 46*)

There are three major forms of allergy diets.

1. The **Single Food Elimination Diet**

2. The **Multiple Food Elimination Diet**

These first two diets are mainly diagnostic. They help *detect* which food could be problematic.

3. The **Rotary Diet**

This diet appears to be both diagnostic and therapeutic. It will reveal a food sensitivity and in time may enable some children to eat foods, which previously caused difficulty, without developing symptoms.

1. Single Food Elimination Diet
(*#2, 3, 7, 15, 46*)

The **Single Food Elimination Diet**, in essence, means that at a four day interval, a youngster is purposely fed a food which is thought to cause symptoms. For example, if a suspect food such as milk is ingested on Monday, then the youngster is not fed this food *in any form* on Tuesday, Wednesday or Thursday (e.g., omit **all** dairy products). On Friday, when the child has not eaten for at least three hours, the youngster is again given milk and dairy products. Similar testing can be conducted on Tuesday and Saturday; Wednesday and Sunday, etc.

If a food causes difficulty, *most* reactions would occur within an hour. In some instances, however, certain food reactions are manifested routinely six to eight hours after a problem food is ingested. This is particularly true if a food causes bedwetting, tight joints, ear fluid, or some bowel complaints such as colitis. Some foods affect children for only 10 or 15 minutes. Other reactions to foods last one half to two hours, and on **rare** occasions one piece of bread, for example, can cause symptoms which last for several days (*#31*).

A mother should try to **check suspect foods on weekends or after school,** rather than in the morning, so that she personally can observe her child's response. Check with your child's physician if any food or aspect of this diet is of special concern.

2. Multiple Food Elimination Diet
(*#2, 3, 7, 15, 46*),

The second major diet which detects food sensitivities is the **Multiple Food Elimination Diet.** If there are several "nails in a shoe and only one is removed, the other nails will continue to cause a limp." If a person has several food sensitivities, and only one problem food is removed from the diet, there may be little evidence of improvement.

During the **first week** of this diet, most fruits, vegetables, and meats can be eaten. Common allergenic foods such as milk, wheat, egg, sugar, corn, food coloring, cocoa, peanut, orange and preservatives are not allowed. Older children should delete tea, coffee, cola and tobacco. Many of these foods have been known to cause a wide range of illnesses in some sensitive individuals. This simple diet can benefit many children who have multiple food sensitivities so that they improve within three to seven days.

To help parents evaluate this diet, they should make a list of all their child's symptoms and complaints. Grade each one as + for slight, +++ for severe, or ++ for anything in between. Record others, such as headaches, abdominal pain or tantrums as once or twice a day. If this is done before the diet is begun, and again at the end of the first week, it is easy to determine exactly which aspect of a child's health was or was not helped by the diet.

During the **second week** of the dietary trial (see Illustration 17), each of the previously deleted foods can be returned to the diet, one at a time. For example, on Monday the child ingests the foods eaten during the previous week *plus* a large amount of milk and dairy products. If there are no adverse effects from the milk, on Tuesday the child ingests a large amount of wheat products such as crackers. On Wednesday, the child would add eggs back into the diet. Each day a different food, which had been avoided during the previous week, is added back into the diet. In this manner, it is sometimes possible to pinpoint the exact foods that are causing each specific medical symptom. For example, a teacher might notice that a child appeared to learn well *until* Thursday when sugar was added back into the diet. This would suggest that sugar affected that child's thought processes.

Illustration 17

Second Week MULTIPLE FOOD ELIMINATION DIET

Each day, an excess of each of the following foods is eaten, as indicated below.

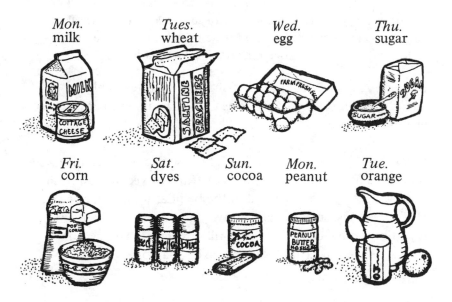

Mon.	Tues.	Wed.	Thu.
milk	wheat	egg	sugar

Fri.	Sat.	Sun.	Mon.	Tue.
corn	dyes	cocoa	peanut	orange

SAMPLE
MULTIPLE FOOD ELIMINATION DIET (#2, 3)
First Week

No milk or dairy, wheat, egg, corn, sugar, chocolate, dyes, preservatives, orange and peanuts are allowed.

What Can Be Eaten?

Most fruits (except orange), vegetables (except corn), meats (except ham, bacon, sausage, smoked or luncheon meat or wieners, etc.) and grains (except wheat and corn) can be eaten, as often as desired. See Illustration 18, page 48.

Breakfast: Select rice, rye, oat or barley cereal **without** additives and preservatives (e.g., brown rice krispies*, cream of rice or puffed rice*, cream of rye, old fashioned pure oatmeal, but avoid Cheerios). Sweeten with honey, date sugar, or pure maple syrup. Instead of milk, use water or the juice of any fruit except orange. Put a banana and water in a blender and make banana "milk." Try soy milk without corn such as I-Soyalac or Nursoy.

Lunch: Make homemade soup from most vegetables, chicken or turkey, or fish; sandwiches with rye crackers (i.e., Wasa*, Kavli*), **pure** white rye bread*, rice bread*, or rice cakes* with meat. Use any allowed meats and vegetables.

Dinners: Any allowed meat or fish, potatoes, vegetables or salads with oil (except corn or peanut oil), and vinegar (no mayonnaise with egg).

Beverages: Hot or cold water with honey or pure fruit juice added, a single herb tea, or juices of fruits or vegetables; fresh fruit, such as a banana, placed in the blender with water or ice, plus a sweetener makes inexpensive juice. Some of these or soy milk can be used to replace milk on cereal. Add carbonated water to pure fruit juice to make soda pop.

*Health Food Store

Snacks: On any day all nuts (walnuts, pecans, cashews, filberts, hazel nuts, macadamia nuts), except peanuts, are allowed providing they are known not to cause allergies. Try potato chips, rice chips*, carrot chips*, maple sugar candy, carob, olives, raisins, plums, prunes or any fruit (except orange or citrus); rice cakes or crackers, or rye crackers (Kavli* or Wasa*) with honey.

Sweeteners: Use honey, pure maple syrup, or date sugar*.

Second Week

Each food, which was not eaten during the first week of the diet, should be reintroduced during the second week. A different food is eaten each day, in addition to all the foods which were allowed during the first week. The foods are eaten in the order as shown on Illustration 17 unless some food is known to cause such severe symptoms that it should not be eaten. The effect of each food can be evaluated at the end of each day. For example, parents may have recorded that a child's hyperactivity decreased from +++ to + at the end of the first week of the diet. If the activity level increased from + to +++ by the end of the day after milk was ingested, it would suggest that this complaint was related to dairy products. Similar relationships may be noted on subsequent days, as the other foods are reintroduced into the diet.

When different foods are eaten after a short period of avoidance, they may seem to cause the reappearance of select symptoms which were evident prior to the diet. For example, milk may cause congestion and legaches; wheat may cause abdominal distention, and sugar and red dyes may cause hyperactivity. Some foods may seem to produce no reaction. Each child's response is highly individualized. If families do the diet together, it is not unusual for each member to react in a different manner to the same specific offending food.

---

*Health Food Store

48

Illustration 18

SAMPLE MENU
MULTIPLE FOOD ELIMINATION DIET

Below is a sample of possible menu selections. Suggestions can be rearranged if other combinations are preferred.

	BREAKFAST	LUNCH	DINNER
Sunday and Thursday	Oatmeal (old fashioned mother's oats), Honey, Apple, or Pear and Juice from those fruits	Chicken, baked or broiled, Potato, Apple Juice	Carrot, Lettuce, Cauliflower, Apple, Pear, Chicken, Potato
Monday and Friday	Rice Cereal*, Date Sugar*, Banana, Grape Juice	Fish, baked or broiled, Rice, Grape Juice	Cabbage, Tomato, Spinach, Banana, or Grapes, Kiwi Fruit, Fish or Tuna, Rice
Tuesday and Saturday	Cream of Rye Cereal*, **pure** Maple Syrup*, Peach and Juice, Papaya	Turkey (fresh or **pure** Louis Rich brand), Sweet Potato, Peach Juice	Squash, Cucumber, Pea, Peach, Turkey or Pork, Sweet Potato
Wednesday and Sunday	Rice Cereal* (hot or cold), Honey, Pineapple and Juice	Beef, Potato, Rice, Pineapple Juice	Beet, Bean, Melon, Berries, Fig, Beef, Potato

For more details about the Multiple Elimination Diet, see pages 135-145.

---

*Health Food Stores

3. Rotary Diet
(*#1-7, 16, 20-22, 46, 48, 102*)

This diet simply allows most foods to be eaten repeatedly at a four day interval, but not more frequently. For example, a child may eat chicken on Day 1, beef or lamb on Day 2, turkey on Day 3, and fish or pork on Day 4. This pattern is repeated on Days 5 to 8, and again on Days 9 to 12, etc. Similarly, specific but different fruits, vegetables, grains, beverages, and sweeteners are allowed on different days of the four day cycle. The total result is that each food can be eaten at a four day interval. This enables anyone who watches carefully to quickly detect unrecognized food sensitivities because problem foods *repeatedly* cause symptoms at four day intervals. A child who drinks milk on Monday and cannot think clearly, may do well in school on Tuesday, Wednesday and Thursday when no milk is allowed. On Friday, however, milk may cause problems again with cognition. This should make both the teachers or parents suspicious of milk.

Furthermore, if foods are eaten at this interval of time, it is thought that some known food sensitivities diminish. For example, some foods which previously caused symptoms when eaten in small amounts may be well tolerated in a few months providing they are not eaten more often than every four days.

It is important for teachers, as well as parents, to have basic knowledge about all three types of diets. Teachers not only can help by reporting their observations, but also by noting intentional or accidental deviations from prescribed diets. Some children will swap or sell their lunches to buy appealing "problem foods." This situation can cause confusion for the parents if a child was fine when he left for school but was not behaving in an appropriate manner after school.

All teachers will recognize why these diets could cause multi-faceted problems during snack or party times. Parents must provide appropriate "allowed" snacks so any child with food sensitivities feels as much like the other youngsters as possible.

Lastly, it should be emphasized that the obvious is unfortunately not always the culprit. It may not be the wheat in the bread, but the preservative or yeast. It may not be the apple or orange, but some pesticide used to spray the fruit. It may be milk in the winter because the cow ate moldy hay and not in the summer because the cow ate grass. The composition of cow's or breast milk is dependent upon what was eaten. Some infants are happy and smiling except if they nurse **after** the mother has eaten a food which bothers them.

What Dietary Substitutes* Can Be Used In Place Of Common Allergenic Foods For School Lunches?
(Health food stores carry many of these items.)

In Place Of: *Suggestions:*

Wheat	Try: Rice Noodles	Rice Cakes
	Rice Bread	Rice Crackers
	Oat Bread	Rice Chips
	Potato Flour	Corn Noodles
	Oat Flour	Barley Flour
	Wheatless Rye Bread	Rice Flour
	Cellophane Noodles	Soy Flour

(The use of bleached white flour should be discouraged. "Enriched flour" usually has more nutrients removed than replaced.)

Corn	Try: Any of the above suggestions for wheat substitutes **except** corn products

Cane Sugar	Try: Date Sugar	Fructose
	Honey	Corn Syrup
	Pure Maple Syrup or Sugar	
	Beet Sugar (not available in all parts of the country)	

---

*Recipes for cooking and baking tasty snacks are in the references in Appendix F, pages 116-118.

(We should all try to **diminish** the use of sweeteners in our society. Any form of sugar, honey or corn syrup can engender an addiction for sweets which can lead to both immediate and long term health problems. The same is true of salt.)

Aspartame is the same as Equal or Nutra-sweet. If a product contains Sucaryl, it may also contain Aspartame.

In Place Of:	*Suggestions:*	
Snacks	Try: Nuts	Fresh Fruits
	Carrot Chips	Corn Chips
	Potato Chips	Rice Chips
	Banana Chips	Dates
	Pure, unsweetened coconut	
	Fruit Roll-ups (without sugar, dyes and additives)	
Commercial Baked Goods	Try: Baking with different grain flours (Recipes are contained in some of the books in the reference list.)	
	Avoid the use of yeast in baked goods and breads if molds are a problem.	
Miscellaneous	Try: Peanut butter without sugar or honey (Smucker's for example)	

CHAPTER V

SYMPTOMS RELATED
TO CHEMICAL SENSITIVITIES
(*#1, 6, 12, 33-43, 46, 55, 63*)

Recognition of Chemical Sensitivities

Children with chemical sensitivities often
complain about odors before other
youngsters notice them. They may
state that a particular smell makes
them ill. Other children, ironically,
crave the specific aroma which
makes them feel unwell. They
may like the smell of marking
pencils, glue or gasoline, and
not recognize the affect
these chemicals have on
how they feel or act.
Either an intense dislike
or extreme craving could
indicate a chemical sensitivity.
Affected children frequently have a
history of becoming sleepy, carsick or developing a headache
whenever they ride in a car, bus or plane.

It is not uncommon to have a history of an excessive chemical
exposure **prior** to the onset of odor-related symptoms. For
example, a massive chemical spill, or painting a home or school
could be the initial exposure which precedes the development
of an exquisite sensitivity to *minute amounts of a wide range
of chemical odors.*

Typical school-related odors which can cause symptoms are
discussed in Chapter II, page 25. Common daily school
exposures include duplicating machines, odors from chemically-
treated paper, chemicals used in printing, and plastic furniture.
Odors from major school renovations, or extensive cleaning

during school holidays or vacations might be associated with the onset of symptoms shortly after some children return to school.

Many schools use pesticides routinely to control roaches and other insects. Organo-phosphate, Pyrethroid and Carbamate varieties contain nerve poisons (*#38, 93*). Alternate, safer preparations such as boric acid should be considered for pest control (*# 6*).

Any type of symptom can be associated with chemical sensitivities but the most common include fatigue or hyper-activity, weakness, headache, "a ballooned or fuzzy head", poor recall, joint pains, or leg muscles which can weaken, burn or repeatedly cramp. Some children become dizzy, limp, act inordinately tired, hold their head, appear to be unable to walk, or simply cannot perform normally in school if they are exposed to a chemical odor to which they are sen-sitive. Some develop heart irregularities. Such complaints are frequently erroneously labelled "emotional" when the basis is clearly physical and related to chemical exposures.

Sensitive children who are confronted with an unavoidable chemical exposure should be urged to hold their breath while they attempt to move to a less contaminated area. Temporary mouth breathing can help prevent some brain-related symptoms, such as unclear thinking. Breathing through charcoal masks can be helpful at times because fresh charcoal absorbs odors (Appendix D, page 107).

The effects of sudden massive chemical exposures sometimes can be reversed by the early administration of oxygen. It is also helpful for the child who develops symptoms such as headache or dizziness after a slight exposure to a chemical to which a strong sensitivity exists. Schools which have pupils who appear to be incapacitated from minute chemical exposures may want to consult with their medical adviser. Oxygen sometimes relieves such symptoms if it is administered at three to four liters per minute for about 10 minutes. This may need to be repeated hourly or for longer periods, depending upon the advice of a consulting physician. Some chemically-sensitive children cannot tolerate the odors of a plastic mask, plastic tubing or even the plastic water container used for oxygen humidification. Ceramic masks, special tubing and glass jars are available (Appendix D, page 107). If a school is not equipped for such medical care, the parents of an affected child may be able to provide the necessary medical equipment and permission to help abort or treat such problematic unexpected exposures.

~ Remember ~

The best treatment for such a chemical problem is *recognition of the cause, and avoidance.* Sometimes temporary breath holding or mouth breathing can help diminish brain-related symptoms due to breathing offending chemicals. Regular outdoor recesses during school hours may be helpful for children who are affected by prolonged exposures to indoor chemical pollution. Individuals whose work is affected by these exposures may find that deep breaths of *fresh, clean* air and exercise can help eliminate the effects of some chemical exposures.

CHAPTER VI

RELATIONSHIP OF PHYSICAL OR EMOTIONAL STRESS
TO THE INABILITY TO LEARN

(*#11, 26, 27, 30, 46, 54*)

Most illnesses are worse after an individual has been under stress. Food and chemical sensitivities, or allergies, suddenly may become evident within a few days or weeks after a severe infection, surgery, a move to a different home, a divorce or separation within a family, or the death of a beloved relative or pet. Stress, as minimal as a menses, could sometimes affect some young women in such a way that an item such as chocolate, for example, which routinely produces no apparent reaction, might cause a headache at that time each month. Another typical example would involve a youngster who routinely has no asthma or hayfever until the pollen count reaches 100. If that same child is subjected to a stress, the hayfever and asthma may occur when the pollen count is only 25. Stresses put an extra burden on the body's ability to maintain normal balance, or homeostasis. Teachers and parents may find that unusual sensitivities to ordinary exposures can develop suddenly after serious stresses occur in children's lives.

The emotional strains in a family with one child who is a behavior and learning problem can be monumental. Many parents are on the verge of separation or divorce because of the emotional, physical and financial stresses created by a single child who will not mind, bites, pinches, swears, hits, screams and destroys. These children often have irritability, depression, headaches, muscleaches and abdominal complaints, in addition to typical hayfever, asthma or eczema. The children often can not sleep, have nightmares and wet the bed. They may keep the entire household in a constant state of turmoil by fighting, bickering, crying, and by their negative response to ordinary suggestions related to everyday living.

Siblings begin to act out because they resent the inordinate attention the "difficult" child is receiving. Many parents have unnecessary guilt because on some occasion they spanked their child when the youngster was having an exasperating high at the time when the parent was having a most discouraging, but realistic low. It is not unusual for parents to state that they love their children, but they do not like them. Many mothers are battered by their children because they simply do not know what to do when the child loses control. Baby sitters and relatives may refuse to sit with these children. Schools may refuse to teach them or may want them placed in special classes. Other children may refuse to play with them. The parents live in fear when the phone rings that a neighbor, friend or the principal may be calling again to complain about the child. The mothers often have the impression from their husbands, relatives, and physicians that they are not doing a proper job of raising the child. Many of these children are, and appear to be "angelic" **until** they eat the wrong food or are exposed to dust, molds, pollen, or chemicals. For this reason a family doctor or an allergist, personally unfamiliar with the newer methods of diagnosis and therapy, may have told a mother there is nothing wrong with her child. This reinforces unnecessary guilt.

And to complicate the entire picture, the parents themselves, may have similar medical complaints related to unsuspected food and chemical sensitivities which make them less tolerant than they normally might be of their children's outbursts. All in all, few families can withstand the stress created by a single child with severe undiagnosed allergies affecting the brain.

It is always surprising and most gratifying to observe how the family tensions diminish after the true cause of the child's problems are recognized and resolved. Many families can cope satisfactorily once they understand **why** the child acts the way he does and once they know that help is available. Months to years of unacceptable behavior, however, lead to conditioned responses which are no longer acceptable after the child improves. Family counseling is often indicated and most effective

after the cause of the child's previous difficulties has been eliminated. There is no way, for example, that a child can be evaluated fairly while he is hostile and hyperactive from eating some problem food, smelling a problem chemical or inhaling an airborne allergen.

PART III
SUGGESTIONS FOR TEACHERS

CHAPTER VII

THE TEACHERS' ROLE
AFTER CAUSE AND EFFECT
RELATIONSHIPS ARE FOUND

If teachers detect that a particular food or exposure *appears* to cause a specific change in a child's ability to learn, behave or act appropriately, they have a few alternives.

Teachers can convey their *observations* to parents, who in turn can attempt to confirm the teachers' suspicions. Under *no* circumstances, *should any teacher advise a diet for a youngster.*

Teachers must talk to their associates so that they, also, are aware that certain foods, especially sweets or cookies appear to interfere with some children's school performance. If these types of foods are offered as rewards for outstanding school work, the effect on sensitive children could be devastating.

Teachers should urge parents to check with their child's physician about possible cause and effect relationships.

Teachers should ask parents if there are any *early* or specific characteristic symptom patterns which indicate that their child is about to feel unwell or act inappropriately. For example, a child routinely may develop red ears, wiggly legs and dark eye circles just prior to an episode of hostile or happy hyperactivity.

An Alka Aid*, one Alka Seltzer Antacid Formula tablet (in gold, not blue foil), or appropriate sublingual allergy extract therapy might abort or relieve an "impossible" episode (#1, 3, 5). Teachers need to know what they can do to prevent or treat such reactions. Appropriate instructions and authorization for the administration of these items must be furnished to the school by the parents and the child's physician.

---

*Health food store

Teachers, also, must be informed by parents about additional observations in the home which might be applicable within the school situation. Parents similarly must be encouraged to notify teachers, for example, about any dietary trials.

If teachers detect something in the classroom which appears to bother a youngster, an attempt should be made to eliminate the offending item. For example, if a pet in a classroom causes symptoms, the pet can be removed. If a teacher wears a particular type of perfume, hairspray or aftershave lotion, it would be helpful to discontinue the use of that specific type of preparation. If a child has difficulty sitting directly under a fluorescent light, move the youngster to a seat near a window (*#91*). If a youngster has difficulty due to chalk dust, or the heating system, that child easily can be seated in an area remote from these exposures. If a child seems to have difficulty in one room and not in another, it might be possible to change the child to a different room within a school setting. If the offending item is a synthetic carpet, for example, the child might have to be taught in a room which is not carpeted. If the chemicals used to lacquer lockers or lay new carpets are offensive, some children may temporarily have to use different routes within the school to avoid the problem areas. Merely omitting a favorite food from a child's diet, or moving a child into a different classroom may resolve a previously impossible situation. A child who previously could not sit still long enough to learn, may surprise an experienced, exasperated teacher by performing well beyond anyone's highest expectations.

On rare occasions, it might be necessary for a parent to change a child to a different school, or treat a child with an allergy extract made from the air in a particular school (Illustration 10, page 20). Easier remedies, however, often resolve the majority of obvious food, chemical or allergy-related school problems.

Appendix A, page 89, contains a few suggestions implemented by some progressive school systems which have improved the ability of some children to learn. These changes, for example, have enabled a few youngsters who required home teaching to attend special classrooms in a regular school.

Of course, any teacher's observations should be discussed with both the child's parents and the principal. The school nurse teacher may help the classroom teacher design an observation evaluation sheet for select children so that detailed specific records are available for a periodic evaluation.

Years of unacceptable habit patterns and responses in children cannot be altered overnight. Once the causes of behavior and learning problems are removed or treated with appropriate allergy care, many children will manifest an improved attitude and performance. The favorable response is sometimes noted within a few days or weeks by anyone who knows these children. Once a child has begun to respond to a comprehensive allergy medical approach, counseling may prove to be most helpful, even though it might have been ineffectual in the past (*# 11, 13*). Many children require behavioral modification therapy if they have had years of subtle and overt rejection and discipline because of their unacceptable behavior and performance. Their decimated self-images need all the help they can can receive from those who care. Not infrequently children appear to be unable to remember what they did or said when they reacted to a food or chemical. While this could be denial, some children truly seem to have no recall about their intolerable behavior. When some children react, parents and teachers often comment on their "spaced out" look and inability to comply with sensible requests. Once these children begin to be aware of their problems, both the children and their parents need to modify their previous patterns of response. Counseling and psychological guidance at that time are most essential.

If a child has not learned the basic fundamentals in school, regardless of his present age, remedial "catch up" learning is required. This may entail a special class or individual tutoring.

Parent-teacher associations should sponsor presentations to explain the role of foods, chemical sensitivities and typical allergies in relation to the school performance of some children.

The school library can be encouraged to purchase some general books that describe behavior and learning problems in relation to food and chemical sensitivities or traditional allergens. These books should be available for parents, as well as for teachers, who want to learn more about this topic (Appendix F, page 115).

~ Remember ~

Even some children who have various types of learning disabilities (# 96), including autism (#21, 50, 51, 86) or Tourette's syndrome (# 21, 95), appear to be helped to varying degrees with some of the newer expanded approaches in the practice of allergy. All children, **regardless of their limitations**, should be observed carefully for the types of physical changes and alterations in activities and mood, which have been discussed (#11). Always ask if the *differences* or changes which have been noticed could be related to what was eaten, touched or smelled? Medical problems can be complex and multifaceted. Unusual responses to foods, chemicals or allergenic items might be one major, significant, missed aspect related to a child's problems in school.

LEARNING DISABLED CHILDREN
8 Year Old Child

This 8 year old child was evaluated in 7/78. Three speech pathologists noted that her school performance had abruptly deteriorated to a significant degree. After discussion with her mother it was determined that her allergy therapy had been temporarily discontinued. Her special diet and allergy extract treatments were promptly resumed. The resulting improvement was obvious to the parents and teachers within a few days and documented objectively at the time of reevaluation one month later.

The following chart clearly illustrates how a child's school performance can improve when teachers relate their observations to parents.

Illustration 19

	7/78	8/78
Affect:	unhappy, tired	happier, alert
Attention span:	5 - 8 min.	up to 15 min.
Mental age at 8 yrs.:	5 yr. 11 mo.	7 yr.
Language comprehension:	3/10 correct	10/10 correct
Auditory comprehension:	4 yr. 8 mo.	6 yr. 2 mo.
Developmental sentence scoring:	2.69	3.77

When sugar was ingested inadvertantly, her family noted that within one to three hours she was incoherent, distractable and crabby. These alterations in affect lasted for two full days.

68

15 Year Old In BOCES* Classes

This 15 year old boy's history clearly illustrates how allergies can affect a youngster's school performance. His close relatives had many typical allergies. His early medical history provided a number of clues indicative of both the typical and less frequently recognized forms of allergy.

Until he was about 13 months old he was a "perfect" baby. His mother states that at that time he became extremely irritable and began to have screaming episodes. In the next few years he developed typical hayfever symptoms. He had diarrhea, bloating, abdominal pain and halitosis. By the time he was nine years of age he had daily headaches. At the age of 13 years he had seen a psychiatrist because he was so belligerent, hostile, aggressive, depressed and suicidal.

His school history is significant. By the first grade he had a reputation of being a behavioral problem. By the second grade it was suggested that he be placed in a BOCES program for emotionally disturbed children. In spite of a superior I.Q., he remained in these classes until he was in the sixth grade. At that time, due to pressure initiated by his parents, he was placed in remedial classes for some subjects but in regular classes most of the time. He continued to fight, hit, and could not sit still in school. He walked "through and on" people. He frequently could not stay awake, and could not concentrate. He was expelled for his "insolent" behavior and attitude when he was in the seventh grade. This coincided with the peak of a pollen season. Activity-modifying drugs were tried without success. It was of interest to note that his teachers often stated they could predict the type of day this boy would have by the way he looked.

In May 1983, at the age of 13 years, a psychologist saw him and suggested that he might have allergies. His mother read a book and placed him on the one week Multiple Food Elimination Diet excluding highly allergic foods (*#2, 3*). Within one

---

*Board of Cooperative Educational Services

week the child was "100%" improved. His mother was amazed because he was smiling and singing! His teachers commented upon the dramatic change in his personality, affect and behavior.

During the second week of the diet his mother found that milk caused lethargy and halitosis, eggs seemed to make him cry easily, and sugar caused extreme fatigue. During an allergy skin test for chicken, he developed abdominal pain, refused to talk or look at anyone, cried, curled his body into a tight little ball, and became very irritable. These symptoms subsided after he received the correct dilution of chicken allergy extract (Chapter VIII, page 79).

If he develops some of his previous symptoms, he and his family usually can pinpoint the exact cause. With increased awareness it is now known, for example, that exposure to odorous marking pens cause him fatigue, an upset stomach and a low voice. When new carpeting with a strong chemical odor was placed in the reading room in school, his grades decreased. When an offensive odor permeated the chemistry classroom, his mother said he acted "crazy" and walked out of class. His grades and behavior can deteriorate during the mold season if his treatment for mold spores is not correct. As soon as his allergy extract treatment is appropriately adjusted, however, he improves.

With a Rotary Diet, a home which is more allergy-free, chemical avoidance, and sublingual allergy extract therapy, he has shown remarkable improvement. He remains "95%" improved unless his allergy extract needs to be adjusted. A piece of pizza, for example, which previously caused him to "act crazy," no longer causes difficulty providing he limits the amount eaten.

After his allergy treatment was begun he started to excel in mathematics. In the tenth grade his Regents math score was 99%. He is now taking accelerated math courses and is in a gifted program for students. His disposition is now "300%"

improved according to his father.

After one year on treatment one teacher wrote that "the changes which have occurred in the past year have been gratifying . . . He is a happier person and more pleasant . . . He is in control of himself in a manner he never was, prior to his treatment. He has concern for others around him in different social situations."

Another teacher stated that he had worked with this boy for two years and had seen a great change. "Last year he didn't have much interest in school. He had problems with other students almost every day. This year he is the first student in class and shows great interest in everything he tries. His attitude has changed 180 degrees. He gets along with his classmates most of the time and tries not to have problems. It is a pleasure to work with him this year."

How would this youngster be today if the *psychologist* had not recognized the possible role of allergy in relation to his behavior, personality and school problems? Wouldn't it have been ideal if this diagnosis had been considered seriously when he first began to go to school?

PART IV
THE ROLE OF ALLERGY

CHAPTER VIII

ALLERGY IN RELATION TO ACTIVITY
AND BEHAVIOR PROBLEMS

Some children who have activity, behavior and learning problems also have typical allergies such as asthma, hayfever, eczema or hives. These same children, however, often have some of the following complaints which are infrequently recognized as possibly being related to allergy. These include headaches, legaches, muscleaches, hyperactivity, irritability, fatigue, depression, belligerence, silly behavior, temper tantrums, sleep disturbances, bed-wetting, and digestion problems (Appendix F, page 121). Any of these medical problems can be caused by exposure to typical allergens (molds, pollen, dust, or pets), as well as foods and chemical odors. For example, a food could cause asthma or a stuffy nose, while exposure to molds, dust or pollen could cause hyperactivity or depression. Each child's response can be highly individualized. Regardless of the many possible causes of the above complaints, any one of them can contribute directly or indirectly to learning problems.

Some children do not have the common forms of allergy. They manifest only the less frequently suspected symptoms mentioned above. If a sibling of an allergic child can not learn or behave, consider the possibility that the "non-allergic" child might have a different, less easily recognized form of allergy.

Consideration of these diverse factors may help to explain why some children's school performance does not correlate with their intellectual capacity. Intensive evaluation and exploration of these variables eventually may provide practical, effective, and less expensive methods to help some youngsters.

DIFFERENCES OF OPINION
REGARDING ALLERGY CARE

Most physicians treat allergy in a similar manner. The initial evaluation usually includes a detailed history and a thorough physical examination. The benefits derived from medical care depends, however, upon how well this is done, as well as the attitude of the physician. Significant differences exist at the present time not only in relation to what is considered to be an allergy, but also in both the diagnostic and therapeutic approaches used in the treatment of allergy (*#110, 111*).

The *First Major Difference* of opinion is related to the types of reactions which food allergies can cause (*#5, 46, 105, 106*).

While there is little doubt that foods can cause asthma, hay-fever or hives, many allergists do not believe that they cause learning or behavior problems in children. Dr. Feingold considered the effects of dyes, artificial food flavoring or natural salicylates to be toxic in nature, not allergic (*#10*). Research studies are needed to help elucidate which portion of learning and behavior problems could be related to toxic factors, to unrecognized allergies or sensitivities or to physical or emotional factors.

The frequently quoted food industry subsidized studies, similar to the one by the psychologist Keith Conners, Ph.D. (*#68*), indicate that food coloring plays a minor role in most children's hyperactivity. Other articles, however, indicate serious problems in both the design and the interpretation of Conners' study (*#69, 70*). In contrast, a number of blinded or controlled studies by ecologically-oriented physicians indicate that foods and chemicals do affect how some children and adults act, behave, think and feel (*# 59-67, 76, 78, 80-90, 92*).

Similar differences of opinion exist concerning the specific role of foods and common allergens in relation to recurrent headaches (*#67, 76-79*), muscleaches (*#82*), certain abdominal complaints (*#80*), eczema (*#84*), fatigue (*#85*), bed-wetting (*#48, 62*), and epilepsy (*#87, 88*). Specialists in environmental medicine (ecologists) believe that there are many causes for the latter symptoms. They firmly believe that foods and chemicals, as well as dust, pollen and molds are unrecognized factors in some patients' illnesses which are not seriously considered by many physicians (#4). Ecologists believe than an undetermined number of children and adults are unable to function at their optimum level because these factors are not properly evaluated by the medical profession.

The *Second Difference* **of opinion is related to how food allergies should be diagnosed. Usually they are detected by:**

   1. Diet
   2. Allergy Testing
   3. Blood Studies

1. Diet
(*#1, 5, 17, 19, 46, 105, 106*)

Diet is one well accepted and inexpensive method to diagnose allergy. The way in which the diet is conducted, however, determines whether a food sensitivity diet will be a success or a failure. Diet studies are meaningful only if they are properly conducted. Here are a few examples:

If children are allergic to dairy products and stop drinking milk for a week, they may not improve. The common reason for this is that they continued to eat yogurt, ice cream, butter and cheese.

If a diet is continued for three to four weeks, the body can adapt so that no *"immediate"* symptoms are noted when an offending food is eaten again. The symptoms, therefore, tend to reappear slowly and insidiously so that cause and effect relationships are easily overlooked.

If someone is sensitive to five foods and eliminates only one from the diet, that person will remain ill. Even though one of the troublesome foods was not ingested, the other four continue to cause symptoms.

If a child eats only a teaspoon of a problem food, or a dozen capsules of that food in a dehydrated form, there may be no reaction. It might require a normal *meal-sized* portion of the food in its *usual* form to cause allergic symptoms.

If a child reacts in an inappropriate manner every time bread is eaten, a mother might assume that the cause is a wheat allergy. Such a reaction, however, could indicate a sensitivity to yeast, a preservative, an additive or the lack of a digestive enzyme. Valid observations by mothers or educators often require a physician's help for proper interpretation (page 43).

2. Allergy Testing
(*#2, 46, 47, 105*)

Routine allergy testing is another common method to verify a dust, pollen or mold allergy. Typical allergy testing for many foods at one time by the scratch or needle method, however, does **not** appear to be entirely accurate. Although a definite food allergy usually exists for any food which causes a strong positive skin reaction, this may or may not be true for lesser reactions. A totally negative skin reaction suggests that a food allergy is not present, when a true food sensitivity or allergy may exist.

Routine allergy skin testing **infrequently** detects the type of food sensitivity which causes activity and behavior changes after normal portions of a food are eaten. It also may not detect the cause of some reactions, such as bed-wetting, eczema, or certain types of ear, abdominal, or arthritic pain which tend to occur several hours after a problem food is eaten.

Although routine allergy testing obviously provides some valid answers, newer skin testing methods appear to detect some sensitivities which otherwise would have been missed. Physicians who use the newer methods find that more precise, but time-consuming testing appears to provide accurate answers. Instead of testing for many potentially allergenic items at one time, each allergen is tested separately. It is important that neither the parent nor child know which item is being tested so that previous bias does not influence the way a patient responds to a test. By careful observation of a child during the testing procedure, obvious cause and effect relationships will be clearly evident. For example, a milk extract might produce hayfever, and a mold skin test might cause hyperactivity. These innovative provocation-neutralization methods of allergy testing enable physicians to reproduce many patients' symptoms with one dilution of an extract, and to eliminate these symptoms with another dilution. Movies and videotapes are available which document and record the typical changes which can be produced in many children and adults (*#94-97*).

3. Blood Studies
(*#5, 9, 48, 63, 92, 105, 106*)

Blood studies easily detect which children are allergic to dust, mold, pollen, and some foods. Patients with these allergies usually have a significantly elevated RAST Test (Radio-Allergo-Sorbent Test). Unfortunately, some children have a negative RAST to a food which clearly and repeatedly causes hyperactivity or other symptoms when it is eaten. Some children have a positive RAST to some foods which cause dramatic behavior changes, but a negative RAST for others which consistently cause similar reactions (*#94*). This merely indicates that the typical blood test, which helps to confirm a food allergy, does not always give the final answer. More reliable blood tests are presently being developed, but for now, these tests do not always provide correct or valid proof in relation to the presence of a food sensitivity.

In summary, we confirm the diagnosis of a possible food allergy by a food challenge or diet, an allergy skin test, or a blood test. While these methods are helpful to detect some food allergies, each has weaknesses and can miss some sensitivities which cause children to have persistent behavior and learning problems. Any of these tests also can give fallacious information and, unfortunately, suggest an allergy exists when none is present. In spite of these drawbacks, the final answer in relation to a food allergy is often practical, inexpensive and easy. If a single suspect food repeatedly can be eaten once every five days, and not cause any illness or changes in personality within 1 to 24 hours, it is doubtful that that food is a problem (page 43).

The *Third Difference* of opinion is related to which methods of therapy are most helpful.

Physicians differ in the approaches they use to relieve allergies. Many doctors utilize mainly one or two of the following; others consider each mode of therapy to be essential in comprehensive allergy care. The emphasis varies markedly in relation to each allergist's practice. The following methods of therapy can be recommended:

1. **Changes in home, school or work area**
2. **Changes in the diet**
3. **Allergy extract therapy**
4. **Drug treatment**
5. **Chemical avoidance**

1. Changes in the Home, School or Work Area
(*# 6, 12, 33-37, 39-43, 100*)

Many specialists hand the patient a printed sheet and suggest a few dust precautions. Physicians practicing environmental medicine usually make detailed, specific suggestions concerning **exactly** how patients' homes, schools or work areas can be made more allergy-free, chemically-free and ecologically-sound (*#6, 12, 33-37*). This can relieve some patients' symptoms partially or completely. A child's asthma can be relieved temporarily with a drug, but sometimes a child can be helped on a more permanent basis by making a few sensible changes in the child's bedroom. Why not find out if a child will improve merely by removing the feather pillow, plastic mattress cover, an old moldy mattress, and synthetic blankets and sheets? Sometimes these measures can help children so much that they require less or no medication. If children feel better, they may be able to learn and comprehend more easily.

2. Changes in the Diet
(#1, 6, 21, 46, 48, 105, 106)

Some children have a history which suggests that foods are a major factor related to their symptoms. A diet, individually tailored to their needs, may help these youngsters. If a child becomes hyperactive from orange juice, the problem may be solved by eliminating that food from the diet or treating the patient for orange (#95). Dietary restrictions may be impractical, and at times impossible, if a child is sensitive to, and reacts to several major foods such as milk, corn, wheat, egg and sugar. Fortunately, a combination of a rotary diet (page 49), and allergy extract treatment appears to be helpful for some children who have multiple food sensitivities.

3. Allergy Extract Therapy
(#2, 5, 46, 47, 105, 106)

Some patients appear to be worse when they breathe dust, molds or pollen. Most physicians agree that most patients who have hayfever and asthma are helped by routine allergy extract therapy for these items. Many allergists, however, are skeptical that treatment for these common allergens can reduce some behavior and activity problems. They also may not believe that similar treatment with foods, pets, vaccines or hormones are helpful for any of the above complaints. Ecologists believe that many food and animal sensitivities can be treated effectively with appropriate allergy extracts. They believe that dilutions of viral vaccines are helpful for some patients with recurrent herpes or flu, and that dilutions of progesterone vaccines help females with certain types of menstrual problems.

There is also a difference of opinion related to how an allergy extract medicine should be given and who should administer it. Most doctors agree that routine injections of allergy extract should be administered in a physician's office. These treatments involve a gradual increase in the dosage and strength of allergy extract over a period of weeks to months. When the patient is receiving an arbitrary top dosage, that amount is injected monthly for two or more years.

Unfortunately there is a disagreement about some of the newer methods used to treat children who have allergies. These methods are advocated by specialists in environmental medicine. They enable many patients to **treat themselves**. Adults can safely self-administer injections of allergy extracts, while children are treated with drops of allergy extract under the tongue. (It is similar to taking a nitroglycerine tablet sublingually, or under the tongue, for heart pain. The medicine is absorbed quickly into the blood.) It is ironic that the absorption of a nose spray of ragweed allergy extract is accepted as an innovative new method to relieve hayfever, but absorption of a similar allergy extract under the tongue is not acknowledged by many physicians as being helpful.

Children who use this newer form of therapy may *not* require a series of build-up injections to reach the final treatment dosage. Sometimes with testing, it is possible quickly to find the exact dose which relieves a child's symptoms. The sublingual drops may be needed one to three times a day, while injections of the same allergy extract are required only once or twice every week or two. Some preliminary research strongly suggests that either of these methods can be helpful for some individuals who have the typical or the less frequently recognized symptoms of allergy (*#46, 50, 51, 59-64, 67, 72, 73, 77, 78, 81-83, 85-88, 90, 92*).

4. Drug Treatment
(*#2, 5, 46, 48, 105, 106*)

Traditional allergy treatment tends to emphasize the judicious use of multiple drugs, with or without allergy extract injection therapy. Specialists in environmental medicine adopt an approach which is much broader. They encourage parents of allergic children "to remove the nails from the shoe, not put ointment on the sore." Parents are taught, in great depth, how to recognize and remove the causes of their child's illness, in preference to treating the effect with a wide range of highly specific potent drugs. They believe that changes in the home, diet, and environment are needed by some children so that accidental or unavoidable exposures to allergenic factors no longer cause illness. Their approach attempts to decrease the "total" allergenic exposure to relieve symptoms and the need for prescription drugs. Realistically this ideal, of course, is not always possible, but for many children it appears to provide an improved quality of health and life.

Educated parents are grateful that they no longer feel helpless. They quickly learn to recognize "why" their children suddenly become ill or act inappropriately. Once they see improvement after changes are made in the diet and home environment, they can make the types of decisions which promote long term wellness rather than chronic illness within their family.

5. Chemical Avoidance
(#6, 12, 46, 55, 56, 93, 105, 106)

Some children's symptoms seem to worsen after exposure to chemicals. Modern chemicals surround us. Allergists have confirmed, for example, that salad bar sulfites can cause severe asthma in some patients. Air pollutants have been proven to cause rashes and breathing problems. These items, however, represent only the beginning of the list of chemicals which should be investigated. We need to know exactly how the minds, as well as the bodies of children and adults are affected by chemicals. We need to know much more about the short and long term effects of the chemicals we breathe, drink, eat and wear.

Ecologists are aware and extremely concerned about the many chemicals in our environment. While some of the effects from chemicals are toxic, others are not. Ecologists can produce and eliminate some patient's chemically-related symptoms with new allergy testing methods. More studies are urgently needed in this area as well.

In the meantime, children must be taught how to keep away from chemicals which are known to bother them. They must learn what to do about unavoidable exposures (pages 54, 55). Everyone must become more aware of the effects of the many chemicals which abound in our food, water, schools, homes, work areas, and outside air.

For The Skeptics
(#4, 5, 105)

The skeptics who chose not to believe that some foods and allergenic substances cause activity and learning problems, must ask themselves the following:

- Why are abnormal responses consistently noted when certain children eat a problem food or are exposed to typical allergens such as molds (#1, 5, 9, 83, 94, 95, 97)?

- Why do some children improve if they avoid eating known problem foods or being exposed to allergenic substances such as dust or molds (#1, 5, 9, 44-49, 60, 72, 82, 85)?

- Why can the specific symptoms which bother some children be reproduced so often and easily when a tiny drop of allergy extract is placed in the skin or under the tongue (#94-97)?

- Why can the symptoms caused by an allergy skin test so frequently be eliminated by giving a weaker or different dilution of the same allergy extract in the skin or under the tongue (#94, 95, 97)?

- Why can some children eat problem foods or safely be exposed to offending allergens which previously caused symptoms **after** they have been treated with allergy extracts (#5, 9, 21, 46-48, 61, 62, 64, 67, 72, 77)?

- Why does the writing or drawing of children change when they eat a food to which they are sensitive or when they are skin tested for certain allergenic substances (*#95*)?

- Why do brain waves, or electroencephalograms, change when some patients eat problem foods or are tested with certain allergy extracts (*#83, 87, 88*)?

- Why do the levels of certain neurotransmitters (chemicals in the brain which transmit nerve impulses) appear to change during reactions caused by the ingestion of certain foods or by food allergy testing (*#9, 63, 92, 94*)?

The fact that medical scientists cannot adequately explain why the above happens does not negate the observations, prove that it does not happen or indicate that the newer approaches are not beneficial. It does, however, indicate a significant void in the understanding of the modern variations used in the treatment of allergic medical problems. At the present time there is more than enough evidence to indicate that large scale, rigidly designed, **impartial** scientific studies need to be conducted.

Although the medical literature early in this century described many of the observations discussed in this book, most physicians, including allergists, were never taught that environmental factors and foods can change children's behavior or activity level. If physicians refuse to give serious consideration to either the current positive medical literature, or teachers' and parents' observations, parents may need to secure the help of a physician who is knowledgeable in the treatment of environmentally-related illness (Appendix D, page 110).

~ Remember ~

Unfortunately the five year olds of today cannot wait 10 or 15 years for large-scale properly executed scientific studies - neither can the 15 year olds who needed recognition of their true problem many years ago. The information in this book, can help some of these children — safely and easily — now!

SUMMARY

The information in this book may help teachers and parents detect the subset of children who are unable to learn because they have unrecognized sensitivities to foods, chemical odors, or unusual, unsuspected allergic reactions to dust, pollens, molds or pets. Knowledgeable caring teachers and parents can learn to recognize the subtle and obvious changes in a child's physical appearance which often precede or accompany alterations in a child's capacity to learn. Increased awareness will enable both teachers and parents to pinpoint possible cause and effect relationships. Simple continued observations may enable those who are concerned to confirm their suspicions. Practical solutions can resolve some learning problems promptly, if there is appropriate intervention by parents, teachers and physicians. Not uncommonly these children are erroneously labelled or treated as if they are dumb, lazy, nasty, irritable, vulgar, belligerent or a "pain in the class." Those who read this book are in a position to alter the course of some children's lives in a positive direction. The initiation of meaningful measures eventually should enable some children to learn and behave in an appropriate manner. The rewards for such a contribution to a child's present and future are immense.

PART V

SUMMARY APPENDICES

APPENDIX A

Suggestions For In-Service School Conferences

APPENDIX B

Suggestions For Parent-Teacher Conferences

APPENDIX C

What Else Can Parents Do?

APPENDIX D

Source References

APPENDIX E

Pollen Calendar

APPENDIX F

Bibliography

APPENDIX A

SUGGESTIONS FOR IN-SERVICE SCHOOL CONFERENCES

Below are some discussion topics that could be used for faculty
in-service programs, parent-teacher conferences, P.T.A.* or
other meetings. In relation to each particular school, the
teachers might ask if there is anything unusual about the educational facility in which they teach. Try to relate each of the
following to the few children in the school who repeatedly
present a special problem.

1. Are there any potential problem areas within the school
   (e.g., floors with synthetic carpets, damp or moldy areas,
   dusty rooms, sections with unusual odors, freshly painted
   or newly constructed areas)?
2. Are there any special problem times during the day within
   the school such as after morning snacks, after lunch, after
   parties?
3. Are there any special contacts, classrooms or types of
   studies associated with more learning or activity, and behavior
   problems than other areas (e.g., lavatories, school buses, lunch
   rooms, chemistry lab, cooking, art class, printing class)?
4. Are there any special activities that appear to cause unacceptable changes in certain pupils (e.g., the use of mats in gym,
   outside gym or swimming)?
5. Are there any special odors inside or outside the school
   which might be affecting pupils?
6. Could unusual situations within a school related to pets,
   heating, paneling, plastic or chemicals be a problem?
7. Have some children's personality or intellectual capacity
   been altered after being taught in a "portable" classroom?
8. Are there any specific children who appear to manifest a
   number of the allergic facial characteristics or types of be-

*Parent-Teacher Association

havior which have been described? Do any children repeatedly complain of abdominal discomfort, headaches or muscleaches? Do any repeatedly wiggle their legs?

9. Do some teachers markedly disagree about the behavior, activity and learning potential of a particular youngster? Does the one teacher instruct prior to lunch, and the other after lunch? Is there a difference in the rooms in which the teachers educate? Does one teacher wear perfume or smell of tobacco? Is there any way in which the differences manifested in a child can be related to either the area in which the child is taught, or to a contact or exposure within that room?

10. Are there any students in the classroom who excel at some times, but not at others? Do the "Dr. Jekyll-Mr. Hyde" youngsters appear to disrupt any particular classroom at a particular time?

11. Do some children unexpectantly do poorly if their examinations are freshly printed on chemically-treated paper?

12. Are there any students who have high I.Q.'s but low academic performance? Can any pupil's inadequate school work be attributed to anything in particular? Are there any children who learn poorly during pollen seasons or on damp days?

13. Do any problem pupils repeatedly come to school with doughnuts, pop, gum, candy and ice cream? Are there any "poor" students who routinely frequent the nearby "junk food" stores or restaurants?

14. Could some children be sensitive to the odor of tobacco smoke? Do any children change in any manner after smoking, leaving a smoky lavatory or after sitting near a child whose clothing smells of smoke (#30, 92)?

15. Do any children act "differently" for several weeks after pesticides are used in the school (#93) ?

16. Are there any children with obvious typical allergies who also manifest behavior and learning problems which have been unexplained?

17. Are there any children with severe learning problems who have no obvious allergies, although there are typical allergies in **other** family members?

18. Are there any children who are particularly destructive or aggressive? Do they have an allergic appearance (*#3, 44*)?

19. Have school guidance or health records given any clues to the source of the difficulty for some children? Did anyone check?

20. Discuss any children whose performances are not acceptable. Decide which teachers can observe these children and determine what needs to be monitored to detect the onset of an allergic reaction in each child.

21. Discuss what options the educational system realistically can provide to help children who are affected by factors in the school environment.

22. Lastly, are there any teachers who feel their health is adversely affected in any way by some of the factors which are problematic for some children?

Possible Special Topics For Discussion

Regarding a "**clean**" *classroom*
(*#6, 33-39, 93*)

One progressive school in Ontario, Canada, has attempted to evaluate education and cost effectiveness related to the recognition of environmental illness and its detrimental effect on learning. The Waterloo County Board of Education in Kitchener, Ontario, decided to try a "clean oasis-type" classroom to therapeutically relieve symptoms in both students and teachers who have chemical sensitivities. With "expert" advice, a special "clean" room was included in the construction plans when an addition was being built onto a pre-existing high school.

Every effort was made to decrease the chemical exposure within this room. The basic principle is similar to the "clean oasis" recommended for the bedroom of some children who have ecologic illness. The classroom has a limited access entrance, electric heat, and is separated from the rest of the school by fire doors. It is lighted by full spectrum lights, contains no plastic, no carpets, no synthetic curtains or drapes, no pets, no odorous art supplies, and no chemically-treated paper. No one who smells of perfume, tobacco or chemicals, in any form, is allowed in the room.

A special air purifier, air conditioner, and dehumidifier were installed to help reduce pollen, molds, dust, and chemical odors.

The children do not write on chalkboards with chalk, but rather on white porcelain on steel boards with water soluble markers.

Some of the environmentally hypersensitive students attend regular classes but if a chemical odor or contact is interfering with their ability to function appropriately in school, they are allowed to go into the special "clean room." It has been noted that this room enables some sensitive pupils to function at a higher academic level. Some pupils find this room most helpful during examinations, damp weather or when the pollen or pollution levels are especially troublesome. Teachers or secretaries who realize they are in some way incapacitated by a chemical exposure also can find some respite in this room.

The room, also, can be used diagnostically to see if a student's activity, behavior or ability to learn is altered by a less-allergenic, less-contaminated or less-polluted area. This type of classroom, however, would not be expected to drastically alter the capabilities of children whose major problems are related to food sensitivities. Children who have combined food, chemical, mold, and pollen problems might find such a room beneficial because the total load of troublesome exposures would be reduced in the cleaner environment.

A few teenage students who previously required home instruction are now able to receive their education within this classroom. Because of this, and other evidence of help during this preliminary pilot trial, the Waterloo County Board of Education is building a second "clean" classroom at their newest secondary school — Jacob Hespeler in Cambridge,

Ontario. They are also making plans to extend their program to include younger students who appear to be sensitive to chemicals.

The construction of the special "clean" room costs approximately $10,000. The following will convey some of the obvious advantages of this approach. Prior to the "clean" classroom, eight students received *three* hours of home teaching per school day at a cost of $16,000 per year. After the room was in use, these eight students could attend school *full time*. The school district saved approximately $6,000 the first year, and will save at least an estimated $16,000 in subsequent years because maintenance costs are negligible. Other students, who previously would have required home teaching, are now able to be taught in school. Because of this room, there has been a significant increase in both the school attendance and the scholastic ability of the youngsters who have utilized the room.

If the possibility of creating an environmentally "clean" classroom within your school system is to be considered, written advice concerning how to construct such areas is available from: Waterloo County Board of Education, PO Box 68, Kitchener, Ontario, Canada N2G 3X5. 519-742-1751. (#36, 37)

Rigidly designed scientific studies are needed to determine the incidence and degree to which the school performance of some children is compromised by an unsatisfactory educational environment.

Regarding a **nutrition** *program*

Some school systems have instituted more nutritious lunch programs after teachers and parents have insisted that these be implemented. In some schools, junk foods in vending machines have been replaced with wholesome snack foods. Some schools allow children to make themselves salads and their own peanut butter. They allow no additives, preservatives or artificial food coloring. They do not encourage children to drink milk if they dislike it.

In his book and in the *International Journal for Biosocial Research,* Alex Schauss has reported several studies which indicate that delinquency and vandalism in schools has diminished, while scholastic ability has increased, when school lunch programs and home diets are made more nutritious (*#44*).

Barbara Reed, a former probation officer, has found that some delinquent children have markedly improved behavior, and can live by the standards in our society if they eat correctly (*#45*). Children on probation, for example, tend not to eat breakfast. They eat more sugar and carbohydrates, drink more milk, and eat less fruit, vegetables and meat than the average child. The role of the diet, in relation to behavior as well as learning, needs more critical evaluation and consideration.

Sara Sloan, from the Fulton County School System in Atlanta, Georgia, has taught the Nutra Lunch Program* in many school districts throughout the United States. This entails not only a better lunch program but also includes an extensive nutritional education program for school-aged children. Grade School #47 in Crystal Lake, Illinois, for example, started this program. It was so successful that state grants were made available to other nearby school districts to try similar programs. Teachers might want to consider the possibility of instituting a more nutritious food program in their present school.

Susan E. Brown, Ph.D. in medical anthropology, is a nutrition consultant who offers nutritional education and comprehensive diet analysis. She can make the rotary diet and yeast-free diet more pleasant, practical and rewarding; and also help with meal planning. In particular, she can help with non-sugar desserts and tasty foods made from various grains. She can be contacted at 1200 Genesee Street, Suite 310, Syracuse, NY 13210, 315-471-0264.

---

*Nutra, Sara Sloan, P.O. Box 13825, Atlanta, GA. 30324

APPENDIX B

SUGGESTIONS FOR PARENT-TEACHER CONFERENCES

Teachers should inform parents about the observations made in the classroom or school setting. Changes in affect, learning or personality related to eating, odors or contacts in certain classrooms or areas of the school should be discussed.

Parents must make teachers aware of known or suspected foods, odors or contacts that have appeared to cause symptoms or changes in their child. If the teacher is aware of the early nuances indicating a potential behavior or medical problem, prophylactic measures can be taken. For example, some children may develop dark eye circles or red ears before they become disruptive. Others may wiggle their legs or have glassy eyes. Many mothers recognize the early "warning" signs. Teachers should know what measures they can take if they notice such changes.

Early in the school year, decisions should be made about the area of a classroom or school that might be least problematic for a child. Some children may need to avoid specific hallways or sectors within a school because of odors or contacts in those areas. Teachers must know if the odor of perfume, tobacco, the cafeteria, lavatory cleaning compounds, classroom pets, chalk or plants are a special concern.

The school nurse and teacher must be informed if any child requires a special diet. Alternatives to the routine school lunch must be considered for children who have food allergies. Some children may be unable to eat in the cafeteria. Where they should eat, and what they can eat if they forget their lunch must be planned in advance. Parents may have to provide special party, snack or lunch foods. Teachers should know which symptoms can occur if problem foods are eaten.

Everyone concerned must know if any medications are needed and exactly when, why, and how they should be administered. The parents should provide the medications, as well as a letter from the physician detailing the child's specific medical problems and needs. In case of an emergency the school must have the current home and work phone numbers of both parents, as well as the phone number of the child's physician.

Parents and teachers must try to anticipate which exposures within a particular school might be problematic for children, and decide if prophylactic measures are indicated. For example, if children are known to be sensitive to chemicals, parents must insist on knowing when and what type of pesticide control measures are to be used in their children's school (#93). Depending upon the type of pesticide, some children may have to remain home for several weeks if the reactions to such exposures are severe.

Close communication between the parent and teacher must continue throughout the year. If a child does not appear to act normally upon arrival at school, or seems to change during the day, the parents must be informed about possible reasons for the difference. This entails careful observation of the exact time when the alteration in affect, behavior or learning was first noted. If a child leaves home well, and acts in a peculiar or unusual manner upon returning home, some discussion is necessary with the teacher to determine what could have caused the apparent change. By working together many pieces of the medical puzzle can be resolved. The key to explain abrupt changes in some children's ability to learn or behave may reside in an increased awareness on the part of both the parents and the teachers, combined with frequent mutual communication.

Parents must appreciate that a teacher's primary responsibility is to teach. They often have large classroooms of youngsters. Many children may have particular needs and require special attention. While most teachers will try to help, some simply will not have the time nor the inclination to observe and analyze. Be grateful and lavish in your appreciation of those who are willing and able to help. **Many times their efforts are over and above what any parent would or should expect.**

APPENDIX C
WHAT ELSE CAN PARENTS DO?

If parents suspect that their child has an unrecognized sensitivity to some environmental factors, the following considerations may prove helpful to verify their suspicions. How much parents might need to do to help their child depends upon the number of factors which influence a particular child's behavior, activity, and ability to learn. To repeat an analogy made earlier, if a child has ten factors which need to be altered, it is similar to having ten nails in the sole of a shoe. A child will continue to limp if only two nails are removed. If a problem is complicated by multiple factors, a family may have to make a number of changes in their life style. Physicians who are particularly skilled and knowledgeable about the detection and treatment of food and chemical sensitivities may be essential. If the problem is simple, however, an apparently challenging complaint may be resolved easily because the "nail" happens to be easy to find and eliminate. A simple diet or a few changes in a bedroom may resolve some children's chronic medical problems or unacceptable behavior in less than a week. Many reference books also are available to help enlighten parents who prefer to try to find their own answers (See Appendix F, page 115).

Parents can try to determine if the causes of their children's learning problems are due to:

- something inside the house (dust or mites, molds, pets)
- something outside the house (pollen, molds, pollution)
- a food
- a chemical odor

Is It Something Inside The Home?

(#6, 33-43, 46)

Parents can suspect that the learning or behavior problem is related to the home if their child is:

- better *when out of the home* (e.g., at school, in a hospital, camping, on vacation or visiting friends)
- worse shortly *after* returning home
- worse when *confined* indoors in the winter
- worse in some *particular* room or area of the home
- worse on the day the house is *cleaned*, or if the child helps with dusting or vacuuming

More details concerning the following will be found in the reference books (Appendix F, page 115).

The *major* offenders *within the home* include: *dust,* the tiny organisms in dust called *mites* which live in stuffed furniture, *molds, pets, feathers, gas, oil* or *kerosene* heat, *scented cleaning items, formaldehyde* insulation, *synthetic* carpets, *plastic* or *vinyl* covered furniture, *polyester* fabrics, and pesticide residues. Pollen is inside the home, as well as outside, during the pollen season.

Simple general suggestions:
- General cleaning: Try Shaklee Basic H*, Bon Ami polishing powder or bar; damp dust floors.
- Polishing: Avoid scented items, sprays or items containing chemicals.
- Vacuuming: Use a type of vacuum cleaner which collects the dust in water, such as a Rainbow Vacuum, or a central vacuum cleaner which conducts the dust directly into the basement.
- Scented items: Avoid *all* types of scented aerosols, sprays, cleaning agents, scouring powders, soaps, toilet paper, facial tissue, hairsprays or deodorants.
- Facial soaps: Try unscented mild soaps such as Basis (drug store).
- Laundry: Use no scented fabric softeners or scented soaps; sun dry clothes, if possible, on breezy, non-humid days. Do not dry wet clothing outside, however, at the peak of a pollen season.
- Bedding*: Buy 100% cotton or wool, no synthetics.**
- Mattress*: Buy 100% cotton, use no rubber or polyurethane. Be sure the mattress does not smell moldy.**
- Mattress cover: *Do not use plastic*; use 100% cotton barrier cloth.**
- Carpet: Try bare floors, or cotton carpets (Penney's or Sears catalogs). Vacuum all carpets well and often, particularly in the bedroom or family room. Steam clean carpets with **non-chemical** cleaners such as Shaklee

*See page 99.
**See Appendix D, page 108-109.

Basic H* and Borax (a mold retardant); try any cleaning product on a corner of the carpet first to be certain it causes no damage.

- Pets: Keep them confined to a room that can be well cleaned. **Acquire no new pets.** Check with an ecologist if you can not part with your pet and your child needs treatment. It is now sometimes possible to treat for some pet allergies.

- Air purifiers: Try those which do not emit chemical odors or ozone (Foust is a good brand*). The room units are fine for bedrooms; furnace units can help diminish dust in entire homes; car units decrease odors inside automobiles.

- Heating: Beware of the leakage of combustion products from kitchen gas stoves or hot water heaters. If you heat with gas or oil or if your furnace is defective, consider a heat pump. *Beware* of kerosene heaters.

- Clean or change the furnace filters at least every 3 months.

- A space electric heater such as "Micromar"* often solves a problem related to forced hot air heating which circulates dust and allows gas or oil combustion products in a bedroom. Close the heating duct or register and seal it with heavy duty aluminum foil if one room is to be heated electrically.

- Cars: Use one with a *recirculating* heat and air conditioning system (e.g., Toyota, Nissan), rather than "fresh" air which circulates exhaust fumes and outside pollution inside a car.

- Clutter: Eliminate as much as possible, especially in the bedroom.

*See Appendix D, page 108.

- Miscellaneous: *Use no non-stick pan sprays or pans; use glass,* not *plastic containers to store food or beverages; use no room aerosols,* no formaldehyde foam insulation; no chemical pesticides or insecticides and no pest strips (*#6*).

Molds are a major unrecognized cause of many forms of chronic and acute illness, especially asthma, hayfever, fatigue, depression and bed-wetting (*#2, 3*). Molds are prevalent both inside and outside the home, on most fruits, in fruit juices, and in or on all cheese, vegetables or nuts.

They are commonly found in older homes, near tubs and sinks, in potting or outside soil, in carpets, mattresses, stuffed furniture, air conditioners, in rooms which contain vaporizers, or in any area which has been water damaged, such as ceilings or basements.

To diminish mold growth (*#6*):
- Use a basic cleaner such as Shaklee Basic G (obtainable from Shaklee dealers — check the phone book).

- Use dilute Chlorox unless the odor is problematic.

- Use 17% aqueous Zephiran chloride (1 oz./gallon water). This can be purchased in a drugstore.

- Borox, such as 20 Mule Team, can be used in laundry to decrease mold growth in damp clothing. Try ½ cup Borax plus ¼ cup baking soda per wash. No other cleaning agent is needed. Sprinkle Borax over moldy areas after cleaning. Vacuum to remove Borax powder from carpets.

- Diatomaceous earth (Agway or pool stores) absorbs moisture from closets or small areas. Some varieties can be used repeatedly after appropriate drying. Read the label.

- Dehumidifiers help diminish moisture and mold contamination in basements. Be sure the water is carried **directly** to a drain.

- Heat or cook moldy foods to decrease mold content. Steam vegetables, cook fruits, bake nuts, broil or cook cheese, heat and then cool fruit juice.

- Open windows whenever possible to increase ventilation and help air out damp areas. Install electric lights to help dry wet areas in the home. An air purifier will help remove molds from the air.

- Eliminate or move house plants or aquariums into an infrequently used room.

Sometimes only one or two of the above suggestions related to the inside of a home will be needed to give a child significant relief.

Is It Something Outside The Home?
(#1, 12, 30, 37, 40-43, 46)

Parents can suspect that something outside of the home is contributing to their child's problems if their child:

- is worse when outside and better when inside

- is worse at the same time each year when pollen or molds are in the air

- has obvious symptoms from outside pollution

- has symptoms from exposure to freshly cut grass or wet, moldy leaves

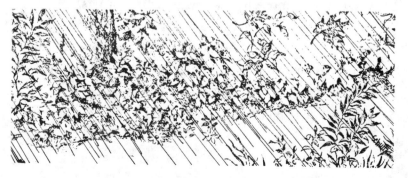

The major offenders *outside the home* include: grass, weeds, wet leaves, *auto exhaust,* expressway odors, weed herbicides, garden insecticides or fungicides, aerial *chemical sprays* for trees or fields, fresh *asphalt* and *factory pollution odors.*

Is It A Food?

(#1-12, 16, 21, 26, 27, 31, 46)

Parents should suspect a possible food problem if their child:

- was a feeding problem during the infant period and then *seemed* to "outgrow" the food problem

- is worse after eating certain foods

- has intense food cravings

- continues to have symptoms regardless of where the child visits or vacations

- has classical allergic symptoms, but allergy skin testing revealed no cause

- continues to require daily medications for allergy in spite of "comprehensive" allergy care

Sick   Well

The diets in Chapter IV may provide fast easy answers. For more details see Appendix F, pages 116-118 (*#16-32*).

The decision to try *any* diet should be discussed with your physician.

Proper nutrition is essential for growing children. Some studies indicate that higher than normal amounts of Vitamins B and C, and some trace metals are required and helpful for some children with learning problems (*#26-28*). Blood studies can determine if the level of nutrients in a child is below the usual accepted normal value. The optimum level, however, for each child can vary and depends upon biological individuality and genetic factors. See page 92 regarding nutrition consultant.

Is It A Chemical Odor?
(*#1, 6, 12, 30, 33-43, 48, 55, 63*)

Parents should suspect odors if their child complains of the symptoms discussed in Chapters II, III and V.

Common sources of chemicals which contribute to some children's inability to learn or behave appropriately are:

- Cosmetics: deodorants, perfumes, hair sprays, aerosols,

men's toiletries

- Cleaning Materials: scouring powders, soaps, waxes, polishes, aerosols
- Laundry Materials: soaps, scented fabric softeners
- Freshly dry-cleaned clothing
- Heating: gas appliances, stoves, furnaces, water heaters, oil heat or spills, kerosene heaters, odorous space heaters, the burning of chemically-treated wood
- Home Maintenance (#6, 33-37): paint, shellac, paneling, plaster, particle board, formaldehyde foam insulation, fumigation or pesticide control chemicals, weed killers, insecticides, fungicides, swimming pool chemicals
- Hobbies: art supplies, ceramics
- Plastic: food containers, mattress covers, soft vinyl "anything," Naugahyde, toys, shower curtains or window shades
- Miscellaneous: scented stickers or toys, chemicals used in sanitary napkins, chemicals used in braces or for care of teeth, artificial food coloring, flavors, additives or preservatives in foods

Diet Records Can Help School Performance

The scholastic or athletic performance of some children is like a "yo-yo" — one day excellent, the next day terrible. If parents will record "exactly" what is eaten on the "good" days, these foods purposely can be fed to these children prior to major intellectual or psychological tests or special athletic events.

Similar "bad days" lists may prove to be equally helpful when children appear to lack cognitive ability. Great care should be taken so that these children do *not* eat foods which appear to interfere with their intellectual or athletic ability at critical times. Some older students find that they think best if they eat only a little of the "right" food prior to an examination. Skeptical older children can be convinced by asking them to pay closer attention to how they feel after they eat their favorite foods. If a student insists that candy, cola, or milk, for example, does not affect his school performance, merely ask the youngster to compare his ability to concentrate or to remember after eating different foods. If a single suspect food is eaten all by itself on an empty stomach, for example on Monday, and not again until Friday, most children would not have any doubt about the effect of that food. Foods tested in this manner tend to cause obvious symptoms within an hour.

The Home Environment Can Help School Performance

The bedroom and home environment of children should be particularly allergy-free and ecologically-sound near the time of important tests. For example, major home remodeling should not be scheduled prior to year-end examinations. The better the diet and home and school environment are at critical times in a child's life, the more a child's performance will reflect his true ability.

105

~ Remember ~

This section was designed to increase parental awareness of the many items which can cause primary and secondary learning problems in some children. It has listed the major factors in a home which might be contributing to a child's illness. If parents become medical detectives they may be able to eliminate the cause of their child's problem. Remember that common allergenic substances (e.g., dust, molds, pollen, pets, feathers), as well as foods and chemicals, can cause much more than hayfever and asthma in some families. While most sensitive individuals do not need to carry out all the measures which have been suggested, the information which has been provided will enable parents to detect many of the common causes of unsuspected and unrecognized learning, behavior, and health problems. Do only as much as you need to do to decrease or eliminate your child's symptoms.

By reading some of the reference books (Appendix F, page 115), it may be possible to help relieve not only some of your child's health problems, but those of other family members. For complicated sensitivities in children or families, the help of an allergist or physician who specializes in the detection and treatment of food or chemical sensitivities, in addition to typical allergies may be needed (#46). These physicians practice environmental medicine or clinical ecology. Practitioners of clinical ecology maintain that a broad range of common physical and psychological disorders can be triggered in susceptible individuals by chemicals, common foods, dust, molds, pollen, and pets. They stress that prevention of illness should be a physician's major concern and that an attempt should be made to detect the specific causes of every medical complaint. Some otolaryngologists practice a similar type of medicine (Appendix D, page 110). For the name of the nearest specialist write to: American Academy of Environmental Medicine
P.O. Box 16106
Denver, CO. 80216

Parents also should be aware that some states, such as New York, have guidelines regarding the special education services which are available for children who are classified as educationally handicapped.

Write for:

YOUR CHILD'S RIGHT TO AN EDUCATION: A Guide For Parents of Children With Handicapping Conditions in New York State.

This booklet is available through:

> The University of the State of New York
> The State Education Department Offices for Education
>   of Children with Handicapping Conditions
> Albany, N.Y. 12234

If you live outside of New York, contact your local or state Board of Education to determine what services for special education are available in your state.

APPENDIX D
SOURCE REFERENCES

Read every label *very carefully*. A food which is labeled dye free and preservative free, may contain additives. A 100% cotton sheet may not need ironing because it is chemically treated. That chemical might be a problem for some children.

Below are a few addresses of places where specific items can be purchased. These are said to be helpful for some persons who have allergies, but the list represents only a few of the many products or places which provide suitable materials. Try to find the exact product which fulfills your particular requirements.

GENERAL SUPPLY
Such as: Charcoal or ceramic masks, etc.
— Allergy Product Directory
  P.O. Box 640, Menlo Park, CA 94026-0640, 415-322-1663
— The Living Source
  3500 MacArthur Drive, Waco, TX 76708, 817-756-6341
— AFM Enterprises
  1140 Stacy Court, Riverside, CA 92507, 714-781-6861

PEAK FLOW METERS
— Assess Peak Flow Meter, Healthscan Products, Inc.
  Upper Montclair, NJ 07043 (approximate cost $19.95 + tax)
  1-800-322-0666

ORGANIC VEGETABLES, FERTILIZER, DIATOMACEOUS EARTH
— Oak Manor Farms
  RR1, Tavistock, Ontario, Canada NOB 2RO, 519-662-2385

CELLOPHANE BAGS
— Erlanders
  P.O. Box 106, Box NN, Altadena, CA 19001, 213-797-7004

ALLERGY-FREE COSMETICS

— Most large chain drug stores or better department stores.

ARCHITECTURE

— For allergy-free residences, Dona Schrier, (Designer), Dona Designs, 825 Northlake Drive, Richardson, TX 75080. 214-235-0485

HEATING

— Micromar, The Heat Machine Plus, Model HM6-4000 Middlebert Road, Romulus, MI 48174 (approximate cost $139.00 + tax)

AIR PURIFIERS

— Allermed 631 J Place, Plano, TX 75074

— E.L. Foust Co., Inc. P.O. Box 105, Elmhurst, IL 60126

VACUUM CLEANERS (Central Vacuum)

— Rainbow System (Jin Rovito, 716-759-2090; Ray Ratliff, 214-250-0525)

— Vita Vac Vacuums (Joe Sulak, 800-848-2649)

COTTON MATTRESSES AND PILLOWS

— Otis Bedding Co. 367 Hamburg St., Buffalo, NY, 716-833-6712

COTTON OR WOOL CARPETS

— Penney's or Sears' catalogs; or Spiegel, 1040 W. 35th St., Chicago, IL 60609

WOOL MATTRESSES, FUTONS, COMFORTERS, YARNS

— Pure Podunk Inc. Podunk Ridge Farm, RR1, Box 69, Thetford Ctr., VT 05075 802-333-4256

COTTON PILLOWS

— KB Cotton Pillows, Inc.
P.O. Box 57, De Soto, TX 75115, 214-223-7193

THE COTTON PLACE

P.O. Box 59721, Dallas TX 75229, 214-243-4149

SEALANTS, STAINS, CLEANING PRODUCTS

— Pace Chemicals Industries
Thousand Oaks, CA 91360, 805-496-6224

VITAMINS

Dyes, corn, yeast, sugar, and flavors found in some vitamins can cause symptoms in some children. Read labels. If the ingredients in vitamins cause symptoms, try a reliable brand from a health food store that does not contain any of these substances. A few excellent brands are:

— Vital Life
Klaire Laboratories, Inc.
P.O. Box 618
Carlsbad, CA 92008
619-744-9680

— Nutricology, Inc.
400 Predo St.
San Leandro, CA 94577
415-639-4572
1-800-782-4274

—

Vitaline
722 Jefferson Ave.
Ashland, OR 97520
503-482-9231
1-800-648-4755

— Da Vinci
(Food Science Label)
20 New England Drive
Essex Junction, VT 05452

— Carlson Lab
Carlson Division of J.R.
Arlington Hts., IL 60004

— Nature's Plus
10 Daniel St.
Farmingdale, NY 11735

— Wm. T. Thompson Co.
Carson, CA 90745

— Bronson Pharmaceuticals
4526 Rinetti Lane
La Canada, CA 91011

— Pain & Stress Therapy Center
5282 Medical Drive
Suite 160
San Antonio, TX 78229

MEDICINES

Ask for white tablet medications and crush them. Be sure to ask the pharmacist if the white tablet has any added dyes or flavors. Remove granules from colored capsules and place them in applesauce, or mashed potato. Avoid colored liquid medicines which contain dyes, sugar, corn and artificial flavors.

Antibiotics

White Tablets: Spectrobid, Trimethoprine-Sulfamethoxazole, (Bactrim D.S.), EES Chewable, Pentids, E-mycin 333, Penicillin, Amoxicillin, Ceftin.

White Granules: Keflex, Pen-VeeK, Amicil, Mysteclin F Capsules, Tetracycline.

Antihistamines

Colorless Liquids: Ryna, Tacaryl, Tavist, Rhinosyn, Hismanal.

White Tablets: Actifed, Tavist, Tavist 1, Tavist D, Rynatan (long-acting), Sudafed, Seldane.

White Granules: Isochlor, Benadryl, Novafed A., Bromfed.

Anti-asthmatic Medicines

Colorless Liquids: Slophyllin GG, Marax DF, Quibron.

White Tablets: Alupent, Marax, Bricanyl, Proventil, Theodur, Brethine, Resbid, Uniphyl, Slophyllin, Theolair SR, Sustaire, Tedral, Ventolin Tablets, Theochron.

White Granules: Theodur Sprinkles, Slo-Bid, Slophyllin, Theo-24.

ECOLOGISTS

Specialists in environmental medicine:

— American Academy of Environmental Medicine
   P.O. Box 16106, Denver, CO 80216

EAR SPECIALISTS (OTOLARYNGOLOGISTS)

Practicing environmental medicine:

— American Adacemy of Otolaryngology
   1101 Vermont Avenue, Suite 302
   Washington, DC 20005

APPENDIX E
POLLEN CALENDAR (*#2*)

The graph on pages 112-114 will enable you to determine the time of the year when tree, grass, or weed pollens are evident in your area of the country. Call your local health department for information regarding moldy or highly polluted areas in the vicinity of your home.

Pollen calendar from J.M. Sheldon, R.G. Lovell, K.P. Matthews. *A Manual of Clinical Allergy,* 2nd.ed., 1967. W.B. Saunders, pp. 342-343. Used by permission.

State	Jan.	Feb.	March	April	May	June	July	Aug.	Sept.	Oct.	Nov.	Dec.
ALABAMA		TREE										
Montgomery					GRASS							
								RAGWEED				
ARIZONA			TREE							RAGWEED		
Phoenix						GRASS						
			RAGWEED		AMARANTH							
							RUSS. THISTLE-SALT BUSH					
Kingman									RAGWEED			
ARKANSAS		TREE										
Little Rock					GRASS							
								RAGWEED				
CALIFORNIA				TREE			RAGWEED-SAGE					
Northwestern					GRASS							
					CHENOPOD-SALT BUSH							
		TREE					RUSSIAN THISTLE					
Southern						GRASS						
								RAGWEED-SAGE				
San Francisco Bay				TREE			RAGWEED-SAGE					
						GRASS						
					DOCK-PLANTAIN							
COLORADO				TREE				SAGE				
Denver							RUSSIAN THISTLE-KOCHIA					
						GRASS	RAGWEED					
CONNECTICUT				TREE								
					GRASS							
								RAGWEED				
DELAWARE				TREE								
					GRASS							
								RAGWEED				
DIST. OF COLUMBIA				TREE								
Washington					GRASS							
								RAGWEED				
FLORIDA		TREE										
Miami			GRASS						GRASS			
						RAGWEED						
			TREE									
Tampa	GRASS											
									RAGWEED			
GEORGIA		TREE										
Atlanta					GRASS							
								RAGWEED				
IDAHO				TREE				SAGE				
Southern							RUSS THIS -SALT BUSH					
						GRASS	RAGWEED					
ILLINOIS				TREE								
Chicago						GRASS						
								RAGWEED				
INDIANA				TREE								
Indianapolis					GRASS							
								RAGWEED				
IOWA				TREE								
Ames						GRASS						
								RAGWEED				
KANSAS			TREE									
Wichita					GRASS		RUSS. THIS. AMAR.					
								RAGWEED				
KENTUCKY				TREE								
Louisville					GRASS							
								RAGWEED				
LOUISIANA		TREE										
New Orleans					GRASS							
								RAGWEED				

State	Jan.	Feb.	March	April	May	June	July	Aug.	Sept.	Oct.	Nov.	Dec.
MAINE				TREE								
					GRASS							
								RAGWEED				
MARYLAND			TRFF									
Baltimore					GRASS							
								RAGWEED				
MASSACHUSETTS				TREE								
Boston					GRASS							
								RAGWEED				
MICHIGAN				TREE								
Detroit					GRASS							
								RAGWEED				
MINNESOTA				TREE		CHENOPOD-AMARANTH						
Minneapolis					GRASS							
								RAGWEED				
MISSISSIPPI		TREE										
Vicksburg						GRASS						
									RAGWEED			
MISSOURI				TREE			CHENO.-AMAR.					
St. Louis / Kansas City					GRASS							
								RAGWEED				
MONTANA				TREE				RAGWEED-SAGE				
Miles City					GRASS							
							RUSS. THISTLE					
NEBRASKA				TREE				RUSS THIST.				
Omaha						GRASS		HEMP				
								RAGWEED				
NEVADA				TREE				RAGW.				
Reno						GRASS		SAGE				
							RUSS.THIS.-SALT BUSH					
NEW HAMPSHIRE				TREE								
					GRASS							
								RAGWEED				
NEW JERSEY				TREE								
					GRASS							
								RAGWEED				
NEW MEXICO			TREE					RAGWEED-SAGE				
Roswell						GRASS						
						AMARANTH-SALT BUSH						
NEW YORK				TREE								
New York City					GRASS							
								RAGWEED				
NORTH CAROLINA			TREE									
Raleigh					GRASS							
								RAGWEED				
NORTH DAKOTA				TREE			RUSSIAN THISTLE					
Fargo						GRASS		SAGE				
								RAGWEED				
OHIO				TREE								
Cleveland					GRASS							
								RAGWEED				
OKLAHOMA			TREE				AMARANTH					
Oklahoma City					GRASS							
								RAGWEED				
OREGON			TREE									
Portland					GRASS							
					DOCK-PLANTAIN							
East of Cascade Mountains				TREE		GRASS		SAGE				
						RUSS.THIS. SLT BSH						
								RAGWEED				
PENNSYLVANIA				TREE								
					GRASS							
								RAGWEED				

State	Jan.	Feb.	March	April	May	June	July	Aug.	Sept.	Oct.	Nov.	Dec.
RHODE ISLAND				TREE								
						GRASS						
								RAGWEED				
SOUTH CAROLINA			TREE									
Charleston						GRASS						
									RAGWEED			
SOUTH DAKOTA				TREE			RUSSIAN THISTLE					
						GRASS			SAGE			
									RAGWEED			
TENNESSEE				TREE					SAGE			
Nashville						GRASS			ELM			
									RAGWEED			
TEXAS	TREE								ELM			T
Dallas						GRASS						
									RAGWEED			
						GRASS						
Brownsville								AMARANTH				
			HACKBERRY					RAGWEED				
UTAH				TREE			RUSS. THISTLE					
Salt Lake City						GRASS			SAGE			
									RAGWEED			
VERMONT				TREE								
						GRASS						
									RAGWEED			
VIRGINIA				TREE								
Richmond						GRASS						
									RAGWEED			
WASHINGTON				TREE								
Seattle						GRASS						
						DOCK-PLANTAIN						
				TREE					SAGE			
Eastern						GRASS	RUSS. T. SALT BUSH					
									RAGWEED			
WEST VIRGINIA				TREE								
						GRASS						
									RAGWEED			
WISCONSIN				TREE								
Madison						GRASS						
									RAGWEED			
WYOMING				TREE		GRASS	SAGE					
						RUSSIAN THISTLE						
								RAGWEED				

APPENDIX F

BIBLIOGRAPHY

REFERENCE BOOKS FOR TEACHERS AND PARENTS*
GENERAL BOOKS

1. Randolph, T. *An Alternative Approach To Allergies.*
   New York: Bantam Books, 666 Fifth Ave., New York,
   NY 10019, 1981. $3.95.

2. Rapp, D.J. *Allergies And Your Family.* Buffalo: Practical
   Allergy Research Foundation (PARF), P.O. Box 60,
   Buffalo, NY 14223, 1980. $12.85

3. Rapp, D.J. *Allergies And The Hyperactive Child.* Buffalo:
   Practical Allergy Research Foundation (PARF), P.O. Box
   60, Buffalo, NY 14223, 1980. $9.95.

4. Forman, R. *How To Control Your Allergies.* Atlanta:
   Larchmont Books, 6255 Barfield Rd., Atlanta, GA 30328,
   1979. $3.95.

5. Levin, A., Zellerback, M. *Type 1 - Type 2 Allergy Relief
   Program.* New York: The Berkley Publishing Group, 200
   Madison Ave., New York, NY 10016, 1985. $3.50.

6. Golos, N. *Coping With Your Allergies.* New York: Simon
   & Schuster, 1 Gulf & Western Plaza, New York, NY 10023,
   1979. $10.95 Soft cover. (See page 130, #108.)

7. Miller, J.B. *Relief At Last! Neutralization For Food
   Allergy And Other Illnesses.* Springfield: Charles C.
   Thomas, 2600 South First Street, Springfield, IL 62717,
   1987. $45.50.

*Prices are subject to change.

116

8. Scheinkin, D., Schachter, M., Hutton, R. *Food, Mind and Mood.* New York: Warner Books, 75 Rockefeller Plaza, New York, NY 10019, 1979. $3.50.

9. Philpott, W.H., Kalita, D.K. *Brain Allergies: The Psychonutrient Connection.* New Canaan: Keats Publishing, 27 Pine St., P.O. Box 876, New Canaan, CT 06840, 1980. $15.00.

10. Feingold, B.F. *Why Your Child Is Hyperactive.* Westminster: Random House, Inc., 400 Hahn Rd., Westminster, MD 21157, Book No. 327419, 1975. $7.95.

11. Ilg, F.L., Bates, A.L., Baker, S.M. *Child Behavior: Specific Advice On Problems of Child Behavior.* New York: Harper and Row, Inc., 10 East 53rd St., New York, NY 10022, 1981. $3.95.

12. Mackarness, R. *Chemical Victims.* London: Pan Books Ltd., Cavaye Pl., London, England SW10 9PPG, 1980. $2.95.

13. Kane, P. *Food Makes The Difference.* New York: Simon & Schuster, 1 Gulf & Western Plaza, New York, NY 10023, 1985. $16.95.

14. Hill, A.N. *Against The Unsuspected Enemy.* West Sussex: New Horizon, Horizon House, 5 Victoria Dr., Bognor Regis, West Sussex, England PO21 2RH, 1980. $5.00.

15. Crook, W.G., Stevens, L.J. *Solving The Puzzle Of Your Hard-To-Raise Child.* Jackson: Professional Books, P.O. Box 3494, Jackson, TN 38301, 1987. $17.95.

DIET

16. Powell, D. *Why 5?* A Complete Food Allergy Guidebook. Box 25, Waterdown, Ontario, Canada LOR 2HO, (U.S. $18.)

17. Golos, N. *If This Is Tuesday, It Must Be Chicken.* New Canaan: Keats Publishing, 27 Pine St., P.O. Box 876, New Canaan, CT 08640, 1981. $9.95.

18. Rapp, D.J. *Allergies And Your Family.* Buffalo: Practical Allergy Research Foundation (PARF), P.O. Box 60, Buffalo, NY 14223, 1980. $12.95.

19. Rapp, D.J. *Allergies and the Hyperactive Child.* Buffalo: Practical Allergy Research Foundation (PARF), P.O. Box 60, Buffalo, NY 14223, 1980. $9.95.

20. Rockwell, S. *The Rotation Game.* Seattle: S.J. Rockwell, P.O. Box 1518, Seattle, WA 98115, 1981. $16.95.

21. Mandell, M., Scanlon, L. *5-Day Allergy Relief System.* New York: Thomas Y. Crowell Co., 521 Fifth Ave., New York, NY 10017, 1981. $6.95.

22. Mandell, F.G. *Allergy-Free Cookbook.* New York: Pocket Books, Simon & Schuster, 1 Gulf & Western Plaza, New York, NY 10023, 1981. $2.95.

23. Stitt, P. *Fighting The Food Giants.* Manitowoc: Natural Press, P.O. Box 2107, Manitowoc, WI 54220, 1981. $5.00.

24. Hunter, B.T. *The Natural Foods Cookbook.* New York: Jove Publications, 200 Madison Ave., New York, NY 10016, 1977. $2.75.

25. Oski, F.A., Bell, J.D. *Don't Drink Your Milk.* Glenwood Landing: Park City Press, P.O. Box 25, Glenwood Landing, NY 11457, 1977. $4.95.

26. Smith, L. *Feed Your Kids Right*. New York: Dell Publication Co., Inc., 1 Dag Hammarskjold Plaza, 245 East 47th St., New York, NY 10017, 1983. $4.95.

27. Smith, L. *Feed Yourself Right*. New York: Dell Publication Co., Inc., 1 Dag Hammarskjold Plaza, 245 East 47th St., New York, NY 10017, 1983. $7.95.

28. Bland, J. *Nutraerobics*. New York: Harper & Row, Inc., 10 East 53rd St., New York, NY 10022, 1985. $8.95.

29. Mandell, M. *It's Not Your Fault You're Fat Diet*. New York: Harper & Row, Inc., 10 East 53rd St., New York, NY 10022, 1983. $13.95.

30. Mackarness, R. *A Little Of What You Fancy: How To Control Smoking and Other Cravings*. Glasgow: William Collins, Co., Ltd. Glasgow, 1985. $3.00.

31. Mackarness, R. *Not All In The Mind*. London: Pan Books Ltd., Cavaye Pl., London, England SW10 9 PG, 1976. $3.00.

32. Dworkin, S. and Dworkin, F. *Natural Snacks 'n Sweets*. Emmaus: Rodale Press, Inc., Book Division, Emmaus, PA 18049, 1974. $5.00.

HOME OR SCHOOL AND POLLUTION

33. Rousseau, D., Rea, W.J., Enwright, J. *Your Home, Your Health, and Well-Being*. Vancouver, B.C. Hartley & Marks Publishing House, 3663 West Broadway, Vancouver, BC, Canada V6R 2B8. $19.95.

34. Pfeiffer, G.O., Nikel, C.M. *The Household Environment And Chronic Illness*. Springfield: Charles C. Thomas, 2600 South First St., Springfield, IL 62717, 1980. $21.75.

35. Department of Consumer Affairs. *Clean Your Room. A Compendium On Indoor Pollution.* Sacramento: Department of Consumer Affairs, P.O. Box 310, 1020 N. St., Sacramento, CA 95802, 1982. $15.00.

36. Small, B. *Chemical Susceptibility And Urea-Formaldehyde Foam Insulation.* Goodwood: Small and Associates, RR #1, Goodwood, Ontario, Canada LOC 1AO, 1982. $10.95.

37. Small, B. *Recommendations For Action On Pollution and Education In Toronto: A Report.* Goodwood: Small and Associates, RR #1, Goodwood, Ontario, Canada LOC 1AO, 1985. $10.00.

38. Zamm, A.V., Gannon, R., *Why Your House May Endanger Your Health.* New York: Simon & Schuster, One Gulf and Western Plaza, New York, NY 10023. 1980. $10.95.

CHEMICAL POLLUTION

39. Blume, K.A. *Air Pollution In The Schools And Its Effect On Our Children.* Chicago: Ecology Research Foundation, 505 N. Lake Shore Dr., Chicago, IL 60611, 1968. $3.00.

40. Saifer, P. Zellerbach, M. *Detox.* Ballantine Books, Random House, Inc., New York, NY 1985. $3.95.

41. McGee, C.T. *How To Survive Modern Technology.* New Canaan: Keats Publishing, 27 Pine St., P.O. Box 876, New Canaan, CT 06840, 1979. $2.95.

42. Travis, N. *The Body Wrecker.* Amarillo: Don Quixote Publishing Co., P.O. Box 9442, Amarillo, TX 79105, 1981. $5.95.

120

43. Randolph, T. *Human Ecology And Susceptibility To The Chemical Environment.* Springfield: Charles C. Thomas, 2600 South First St., Springfield, IL 62717, 1962. $9.25.

DELINQUENCY

44. Schauss, A. *Diet, Crime And Delinquency.* Berkeley: Parker House, 2340 Parker St., Berkeley, CA 84704, 1980. $4.95.

45. Reed, B. *Food, Teens And Behavior.* Manitowoc: Natural Press, P.O. Box 2107, Manitowoc, WI 54220, 1983. $7.00.

TEXTS FOR PHYSICIANS AND PSYCHOLOGISTS
ON CLINICAL ECOLOGY AND
ENVIRONMENTAL MEDICINE
(also see reference 7)

46. Bell, I. *Clinical Ecology.* Bolinas: Common Knowledge Press, P.O. Box 316, Bolinas, CA 94924, 1982. $4.95.

47. Miller, J. *Food Allergy: Provocative Testing And Injection Therapy.* Springfield: Charles C. Thomas, 2600 South First St., Springfield, IL 62717, 1972. $16.25.

FOOD ALLERGY

48. Gerrard, J. *Food Allergy — New Perspectives.* Springfield: Charles C. Thomas, 2600 South First St., Springfield, IL 62717, 1980. $19.95.

49. Rinkel, H.J., Randolph, T.G., Zeller, M. *Food Allergy.* Springfield: Charles C. Thomas, 2600 South First St., Springfield, IL 62717, 1951. $49.75.

121

BEHAVIOR AND LEARNING DISORDERS

50. O'Banion, D. *The Ecologic And Nutritional Approach To Behavior Medicine.* Springfield: Charles C. Thomas, 2600 South First St., Springfield, IL 62717, 1981. $24.75.

51. O'Banion, D. *The Ecologic And Nutritional Treatment Of Health Disorders.* Springfield: Charles C. Thomas, 2600 South First St., Springfield, IL 62717, 1981. $24.75.

YEAST INFECTIONS

52. Truss, O. *The Missing Diagnosis.* Birmingham: The Missing Diagnosis, Inc., 2614 Highland Ave., Birmingham, AL 35205, 1985. $8.95.

53. Crook, W. *The Yeast Connection.* Jackson: Professional Books, P.O. Box 3494, Jackson, TN 38301, 1983. $13.95.

STRESS

54. Selye, H. *The Stress Of Life.* New York: McGraww-Hill Book Co., 1221 Avenue of the Americas, New York, NY 10020, 1956. $4.95.

CHEMICALS

55. Randolph, T.G. *Human Ecology And Susceptibility To The Chemical Environment.* Springfield: Charles C. Thomas, 2600 South First St., Springfield, IL 62717, 1967. $18.75.

56. Dadd, D.L., Levin, A.S. *A Consumer Guide For The Chemically Sensitive.* San Francisco: Alan S. Levin, M.D., 450 Sutter, Suite 1138, San Francisco, CA 94108, 1982. $18.00.

SCIENTIFIC REFERENCES

HYPERACTIVITY

57. Rapp, D.J. 1985. Allergies: Are some children pains in the class? Journal School Administrators Association of New York State, 16:29-32.

58. Hilsen, J.E. 1982. Dietary control of the hyperactive child. New York Pediatrician, Summer: 25-29.

59. Egger, J., Carter, C.M., Graham, P.J., Gumley, D., Soothill, J.F. 1985. Controlled trial of oligoantigenic treatment in the hyperkinetic syndrome. Lancet. 1:540-545.

60. Rapp, D.J. 1978. Does diet affect hyperactivity? Journal of Learning Disabilities, 11:56-61.

61. Rapp, D.J. 1979. Food allergy treatment for hyperkinesis. Journal of Learning Disabilities, 12:42-50.

62. Rapp, D.J. 1978. Double-blind confirmation and treatment of milk sensitivity. Medical Journal of Australia, 1:571.

63. Rea, W.J., et al. 1978. Food and chemical susceptibility after environmental chemical overexposure: Case histories. Annals of Allergy, 41(2):101-110.

64. O'Shea, J.A., Porter, S.F. 1981. Double-blind study of children with hyperkinetic syndrome treated with multi-allergen extract sublingually. Journal of Learning Disabilities, 14(4):189.

65. Weiss, B. 1980. Behavioral responses to food coloring. Science, 207:1487-1489.

66. Gerrard, J. 1984. Just food intolerance. Lancet, 2:413.

67. Miller, J.B. 1977. A double-blind study of food extract injection therapy: A preliminary report. Annals of Allergy, 38:185-191.

68. Conners, C.K., Goyette, C.H., Southwick, D.A., Lees, J.M., Andrulonis, P.A. 1976. Food additives and hyperkinesis: A Controlled double-blind experiment. Pediatrics, 58:154.

CRITIQUES OF CONNER'S STUDIES

69. Rippere, V. 1983. Food additives and hyperactive children: A Critique of Conners. British Journal of Clinical Psychology, 22:19-32.

70. Weiss, B. 1982. Color Me Hyperactive. American Health, May/June: 68-73.

ASTHMA

71. Soothill, J.F., Warner, J.O. 1978. Control of hyposensitization to dermatophagoides pteronyssinus in children with asthma. Lancet, 2:912-915.

72. Boris, M., Schiff, M., Weindorf, S., Inselman, L. 1983. Abstract. Bronchoprovocation blocked by neutralization therapy. Journal of Allergy and Immunology, 71(1), Part 2:92.

73. Boris, M., Weindorf, S., Corriel, R., Inselman, L., Schiff, M. 1985. Antigen induced asthma attenuated by neutralization therapy. Clinical Ecology, 3(2):59-62.

124

OTITIS
(also see reference 104)

74. Shambaugh, G. 1983. Serous Otitis: Are tubes the answer? American Journal of Otology, 5:63-65.

75. Rapp, D.J., Fahey, D. 1973. Chronic secretory otitis and allergy. Journal of Asthma and Research, 10:193-218.

MIGRAINE

76. Egger, J., Carter, C.M., Wilson, J., Turner, M.W., Soothill, J.F. 1983. Is migraine food allergy? A double-blind controlled trial of oligoantigenic diet treatment. Lancet, 2:865-869.

77. Miller, J.B. 1977. A double-blind study of food extract injection therapy: A preliminary report. Annals of Allergy, 38:185-191.

78. Monro, J., Brostoff, J., Carini, C., Zilka, K. 1980. Food allergies in migraine. Lancet, 2:1-4.

79. Grant, E.C. 1978. Oral contraceptives, smoking, migraines, and food allergy. Lancet, 2:581.

COLITIS

80. Soothill, J.F., Jenkins, H.R., Pincott, J.R., Milla, P.J., Harries, J.T. 1983. Food allergy: The major cause of infantile colitis. Archives of Disease in Childhood, 59:326-329.

PHYSICAL AND PSYCHOLOGICAL COMPLAINTS

81. King, D.S. 1981. Can allergy exposure provoke psycho-

logical symptoms? A double-blind test. Biological
Psychiatry, 16:3-19.

82. Finn, R., Battcock, T.M. 1985. A critical study of clinical
ecology. The Practitioner, 229:883-885.

83. Sahley, B.J. *The Natural Way To Control Hyperactivity,
With Amino Acids and Nutrient Therapy.* San Antonio:
The Watercress Press, San Antonio, TX 78229, 1989.
$6.95.

ECZEMA

84. Atherton, D.J., Soothill, J.F., Sewell, W., Wells, R.S.
1978. A double-blinded controlled crossover trial of an
antigen avoidance diet in atopic eczema. Lancet, 1:401-403.

FATIGUE

85. Crook, W. C., Harrison, W.E., Crawford, S.E., Emerson,
B.S. 1961. Systemic manifestations due to allergy.
Pediatrics, 27:290.

AUTISM

86. O'Banion, D., Armstrong, C. 1978. Disruptive behaivor:
A dietary approach. Journal of Autism and Childhood
Schizophrenia, 8:325.

EPILEPSY

87. Crayton, J.W. 1981. Epilepsy precipitated by food sensitivity: Report of a case with double-blind placebo-controlled
assessment. Clincal Electroencephalography, 12:192.

88. Egger, J., Soothill, J.F., Wilson, J. 1989. Oligoantigenic diet treatment of children with epilepsy and migraine. The Journal of Pediatrics, 114:51-58.

MISCELLANEOUS

89. Green, M. 1974. Sublingual provocation testing for foods and F, D & C dyes. Annals of Allergy, 33:274.

90. Radcliffe, M.J., et al. 1981. Food allergy in polysymptomatic patients. The Practitioner, 225:1651-1654.

91. Ott, J. *Light, Radiation, & You.* Greenwich: Devin-Adair Publishers, 6 North Water St., Greenwich, CT 06830, 1982. $9.95.

92. McGovern, J.J., et al. 1983. Food and chemical sensitivity. Archives of Otolaryngology, 109:292-297.

93. Anderson, A. 1982. Neutotoxic follies. *Psychology Today*, 16:30-331.

VIDEOTAPES

94. Rapp, D.J. *Do Foods Alter Behavior and Activity?* This tape clearly demonstrates the typical range of reactions which can occur in two, three, and four year old children. The reactions include irritability, hyperactivity, hostility, aggression and fatigue. One portion shows how a child acts and behaves before and after he eats a food to which he is sensitive. Other sectors demonstrate the total change in personality which occurs after children are allergy tested or treated in a single-blinded manner for milk, banana, food coloring and maple syrup. Immunologic data is included.

To purchase write: Educational Communications Center, 24 Capen Hall, State University of New York at Buffalo, Amherst, NY 14260, Attn: Media Library. $75.00.

The following videotapes may be purchased through the Practical Allergy Research Foundation (PARF), P.O. Box 60, Buffalo, NY 14223.

95. Rapp, D.J. *Learning and Allergy*. This three part series vividly demonstrates that some children have learning and behavior problems related to foods, chemical odors or exposures to dust, molds, pollen or pets.

Part 1. In this tape, the obvious physical changes in appearance which occur when a child reacts to common foods or environmental factors are shown. There are characteristic alterations in some children's facial appearance, as well as in the manner in which they wrote, or in the content of their pictures. These clues should help teachers and parents suspect which children might have undiagnosed allergies affecting their ability to learn. Select sequences clearly demonstrate how a child suddenly can have a total change in behavior and activity after eating a problem food or after a typical allergy skin test. This tape demonstrates how quickly these children return to normal after appropriate treatment.

Part 2. This tape dramatically illustrates specific school environmental factors which might repeatedly alter a child's ability to learn. It explains how a teacher or parent can easily recognize some cause and effect relationships. It demonstrates how to detect consistent patterns in children who suddenly cannot learn or act appropriately because of foods or common environmental exposures found both inside or outside of schools or homes. This tape shows teachers and parents how to make the connection and determine if foods, pollen, molds, dust, or chemicals are factors interfering with some youngsters' ability to learn in a manner commensurate with their ability.

128

Part 3. This tape illustrates special types of educational challenges which can confront teachers. These include:

- The easily missed changes which can occur in a learning disabled child after exposure to molds or after an allergy skin test for a mold.

- The type of vulgarity which can be noted in a child who has Tourette's Syndrome when he is skin tested with an extract made from the air in his school.

- A child who was erroneously thought to be retarded and slow until his food sensitivities were detected.

- A typical temper tantrum produced in a nursery school child after he eats sugar cubes.

- The classical reaction seen in a hyperactive, irritable, food allergic infant.

Each videotape costs $90 or $225 for the entire 3 part series.

96. Rapp, D.J. *Impossible Child or Allergic Child.* This 20 minute tape presents the reactions of six children before, during and after allergy testing. Interviews with 3 mothers illustrate the children's problems, and the parents' response. This short tape can be used totally or in part. It is especially useful in demonstrating how unsuspected and unrecognized allergies can affect some children. $75.00.

97. Rapp, D.J. *Why Some Children Can't Learn And Behave.* A lecture for educators. This two hour tape was made during a workshop for educators. It discusses how to recognize school children who might have ecologic illness by their appearance and behavior. This video includes explanatory slides and examples of changes in handwriting and drawing during reactions to various items. It includes many movies which vividly illustrate the changes which occur in some children during allergy testing. $250.00.

AUDIO CASSETTE TAPES

The following audio cassette tapes may be purchased through
the Practical Allergy Research Foundation (PARF), P.O. Box
60, Buffalo, NY 14223.

98. *Infant Allergies.* $10.95 Companion book entitled,
Screaming Infants - Desperate Mothers. Also see reference #133.

99. *Allergy Diets.* $10.95.

100. *Environmental Aspects Of Allergy.* $10.95.

NEW AND IMPORTANT PUBLICATIONS
NOT REFERENCED IN TEXT

101. Franklin, A.J. *The Recognition And Management Of Food
Allergy In Children.* New Jersey: Parthenon Publishing
Group, 120 Mill Road, Park Ridge, NJ 07656, 1988. $58.00.

102. Berger, S.M. *Dr. Berger's Immune Power Diet.* New
American Library, P.O. Box 999, Bergenfield, NJ 07621,
1985. $5.50.

103. Smith, L. *Diet Plan For Teens.* New York: McGraw-Hill
Book Co., 1221 Avenue of the Americas, New York, NY
10020, 1986. $17.95.

104. Boris M., Boris, G., Weindorf, S. 1986. Association of
otitis media with exposure to gas fuels. Clinical Ecology.
3(4):195-198.

105. Rapp. D.J. 1986. Environmental Medicine: An expanded
approach to allergy. Buffalo Physician, SUNYAB,
3435 Main St., Buffalo, NY 14214, 19(5):16, 18-24.

106. Ellis, E.F. 1986. Clinical Ecology: Myth and reality. Buffalo Physician, SUNYAB, 3435 Main Street, Buffalo, NY 14214, 19(5):17, 24-28.

107. Seely, S., Freed, D., Silverstone, G., Rippere, V. *Diet-Related Diseases: The Modern Epidemic.* Westport: The Avi Publishing Co., 250 Post Road East, P.O. Box 831, Westport, CT 06881 or Croom Helm Ltd., Provident House, Burrell Row, Beckenham, Kent, England BR3 1AT, 1985. $9.95.

108. Golos, N., Golbitz, F. *Coping With Your Allergies.* New York: Simon & Schuster, Fireside Press, 1 Gulf & Western Plaza, New York, NY 10023, 1986. $10.95.

ALLERGY TREATMENT BOOKS
(Also see Reference 7)

109. Brostoff, J., Challacombe, S. ed., *Food Allergy and Intolerance.* Philadelphia: Baillere-Tindall/W.B. Saunders, West Washington Square, Philadelphia, PA 19105, 1987. (Rapp, D.J. Sublingual Testing and Treatment, Chapter 56, pg. 961-968).

110. Berger, S.M. *What Your Doctor Didn't Learn In Medical School.* New York: Wm. Morrow & Co., 105 Madison Ave., New York, NY 10116, 1989. $18.95.

ALTERNATIVES TO RITALIN
(See page 146)

111. Sahley, B.J. *The Natural Way To Control Hyperactivity, With Amino Acids and Nutrient Therapy.* San Antonio: The Watercress Press, San Antonio, TX 78229, 1989. $6.95.

112. Schauss, A., Clark, D. *The Legal Drugging Of Children: Children Who Can't Say No.* Tacoma: Life Sciences Press, P.O. Box 1174, Tacoma, WA 98411, 1989. $9.95.

ARTHRITIS BOOKS

113. Fredericks, C. *Arthritis, Don't Learn To Live With It.*

New York: Perigee Books, The Putnam Publishing Group, 200 Madison Avenue, New York NY 10016, 1981. $7.95.

114. Mandell, M. *Dr. Mandell's Lifetime Arthritis Relief System.* New York: Coward-McCann, Inc., 200 Madison Ave., New York, NY 10016, 1983. $13.95.

HEART

115. Rea, W.J. 1976. Environmentally triggered thrombophlebitis. Annals of Allergy, 37:102-109.

116. Rea, W.J. 1977. Environmentally triggered small vessel vasculitis. Annals of Allergy, 38:245.

117. Rea, W.J. 1978. Environmentally triggered cardiac disease. Annals of Allergy, 40:243-251.

118. Rea, W.J. 1981. Recurrent environmentally triggered thrombophlebitis. Annals of Allergy, 47:338-344.

HOUSE POLLUTION

119. Dadd, D.L. *Nontoxic and Natural.* Los Angeles: Jeremy P. Tarcher, Inc., 9110 Sunset Blvd., Los Angeles, CA 90069, 1984. $9.95.

120. Dadd, D.L. *The Nontoxic Home.* Los Angeles: Jeremy P. Tarcher, Inc., 9110 Sunset Blvd., Los Angeles, CA 90069, 1986. $9.95.

MIGRAINE BOOKS

121. Sereda, A.W. *Headache Control Without Drugs.* Edmonton: Amaranthine Press, P.O. Box 8130, Stn.F, Edmonton, Alberta, Canada T6H 4N9. 1987.

NUTRITION BOOKS

122. Galland, L., Buchman, D. *Superimmunity For Kids.* New York: E.P. Dutton, 2 Park Ave., New York, NY 10016, 1988. $18.95. (Also available in paperback.)

123. Smith, L. *Diet Plan For Teens.* New York: McGraw-Hill Book Co., 1221 Avenue of the Americas, New York, NY 10020, 1986. $17.95.

124. Schauss, A. *Zinc Therapy And The Primary Eating Disorders.* Tacoma: Life Sciences Press, P.O. Box 1174, Tacoma, WA 98401-1174, 1989. $8.95.

DIET

125. Mumby, K. *The Food Allergy Plan.* Reno: CRCS Publications, P.O. Box 20850, Reno, NV 89515, 1986. $5.95.

126. Remington, D.W., Higa, B.W. *Back To Health.* Provo: Vitality House International, Inc., 3707 North Canyon Road, #8-C, Provo, UT 84604, 1986. $9.95.

127. Remington, D.W., Higa, B.W. *The Bitter Truth About Artificial Sweeteners.* Provo: Vitality House International, Inc., 3707 North Canyon Road, #8-C, Provo, UT 84604, 1986. $9.95.

BRITISH BOOKS FOR THE PUBLIC

128. Rippere, V. *The Allergy Problem.* Northamptonshire: Thorsons Publishers Limited, Wellingborough, Northamptonshire, England, 1983.

129. Lewith, G.T., Kenyon, J.N. *Clinical Ecology.* Northamptonshire: Thorsons Publishers Limited, Wellingborough, Northamptonshire, England, 1985.

130. Mansfield, P., Munro, J. *Chemical Children*. London: Century Hutchinson Ltd., Brookmount House, 62-65 Chandos Place, Covent Garden, London, England WC2N 4NW, 1987. $4.95.

131. Franklin, A.J. *The Recognition And Management Of Food Allergy*. (How infant allergies can lead to behavior and learning problems.) Parthenon Publishing Group, 120 Mill Road, Park Ridge, NJ. 1988.

BOOKLETS

132. Rapp, D.J. *Recognize And Manage Your Allergies*. New Canaan: Keats Publishing Inc., P.O. Box 876, New Canaan, CT 06840, 1987. $2.25.

133. Rapp, D.J. *Screaming Infants — Desperate Mothers*. Buffalo: Practical Allergy Research Foundation (PARF), P.O. Box 60, Buffalo, NY 14223-0060, due 1990.

ARTICLES

HYPERACTIVITY AND DIET

134. Egger, J., Carter, C., Soothill, J., Wilson, J. 1989. Oligoantigenic diet treatment of children with epilepsy and migraine. The Journal of Pediatrics, 114:51-58.

135. Kaplan, B., McNichol, J., Conte, R., Moghadam, H. 1989. Dietary replacement in preschool-aged hyperactive boys. Pediatrics, 83:7-17.

136. Satterfield, J.M., Satterfield, B., Schell, A. 1987. Therapeutic interventions to prevent delinquency in hyperactive boys. Journal of American Academy Of Children And Adolescent Psychology, 26:56-64.

134

YEAST INFECTIONS

137. Connolly, P. *The Candida Albicans Yeast-Free Cookbook.*
New Canaan: Keats Publishing Inc., P.O. Box 876,
New Canaan, CT 06840, 1985. $9.95.

138. Trowbridge, J.P., Walker, M. *The Yeast Syndrome.*
New York: Bantam Books, Inc., 666 Fifth Avenue, New
York, NY 10103, 1986. $4.95.

139. Wunderlich, R.C., Kalita, D.K. *Candida Albicans.* New
Canaan: Keats Publishing Inc., P.O. Box 876, New
Canaan, CT 06840, 1984. $1.95.

SUBLINGUAL ALLERGY EXTRACT TREATMENT

140. Brostoff, J., Scadding, G.K. 1986. Low dose sublingual
therapy in patients with allergic rhinitis due to house dust
mite. Clinical Allergy, 16:483-491.

141. King, W.P., Wallace, A.R., Fadal, G., Ward, W.A.,
Trevino, R.J., Pierce, W.B., Stewart, J.A., Boyles, J.H.
1988. Provocation-neutralization: A two-part study.
Part 1. The intracutaneous provocative food test. A
multi-center comparison study. Otolaryngology — Head
and Neck Surgery, 9:263-277.

142. Holt, P.G., Vines, J., Britten, D. 1988. Sublingual
allergen administration. 1. Selective suppression of IgE
production in rats by high allergen doses. Clinical Allergy,
18:229-234.

NEPHROSIS

143. LaGrue, G., Laurent, J., Rostoker, G., Lang, P. 1987. Food
allergy in idiopathic nephrotic syndrome. The Lancet, ii:777.

DETAILS FOR TWO WEEK
MULTIPLE FOOD ELIMINATION DIET

MULTIPLE FOOD ELIMINATION DIET

Part 1

How Do You Do the First Part of the Diet?

During the first week, most meats, fruits and vegetables can be eaten. (The "allowed" foods are listed on pg. 138). Keep detailed records in a food diary of **exactly** what is eaten. Most patients who are going to respond favorably to the diet, do so about the sixth or seventh day. Improvement noted as early as day two may greatly increase by day seven. The object is to see the maximum amount of improvement which can be noted during the first seven days. If your child is better in a week or less, begin Part 2 of the diet on the eighth day.

If you want to help your entire family, urge everyone to try the diet at the same time. Typically, several family members will note improvement in how they feel or act when this is done.

If your child is not better within a week, re-check the diet records for the initial week of the diet. Were only the allowed foods eaten? If your child repeatedly forgot and ate the wrong foods or drank the wrong beverages, the item which was not deleted or omitted from the diet may be at fault. Try Part 1 of the diet again, but this time try much harder to adhere strictly to the diet. This fast, inexpensive method of food allergy detection can sometimes provide relief of many chronic medical complaints.

Occasionally, a person is worse during Part 1 of the diet. If this happens, immediately stop the diet. A frequent cause is that the patient has begun to eat an excessive amount of an unsuspected offending food. A child who substitutes apple or grape juice for milk, for example, may act or behave much worse, if apple or grape juice is the cause of these symptoms. Retry Part 1 of the diet, but stop the food which you think made your child worse. You may have already found one answer.

Rarely, a child who was not helped during the first week will dramatically improve with a more prolonged diet. In other words, continue Part 1 of the diet for two weeks, not one week. If Part 1 of the diet is tried and has not helped by the fourteenth day, this particular diet is probably not the answer for your child or your family. The medical problems are not related to foods or are possibly due to other frequently eaten or craved food items; i.e.: mushrooms, cinnamon, coffee, tea, etc.

If an infection occurs during the diet, stop the diet until your child is well. It is too difficult to interpret the results if it is continued.

WHICH FOODS DOES DIET DELETE

During Part 1 of the diet, the following foods are omitted in all forms: milk and dairy products (yogurt, cheese, ice cream, casein), wheat (bread, cake, cookies, baked goods), eggs, corn, sugar, chocolate (cocoa or cola), peas (peanut butter), citrus (orange, lemon, lime, grapefruit), food coloring, food additives and preservatives. No luncheon meats, sausage, ham or bacon are allowed. If there is some question about a specific food, do not eat it.

PART 1 OF MULTIPLE ELIMINATION DIET
READ ALL LABELS FIRST

ALLOWED

CEREALS
Rice — Rice Puffs only
Oats — Oatmeal made with honey
Barley

FRUITS
Any fresh fruit, except citrus
Canned (if in their own juice and without artificial color, sugar, or
    preservatives)

VEGETABLES
Any fresh vegetables except corn and peas
French fries (homemade)
Potatoes

MEATS
Chicken or turkey (non-basted)
Louis Rich ground turkey
Veal or beef
Pork
Lamb
Fish, tuna

BEVERAGES
Single herb or other tea with honey
Water
Grape juice, bottled (Welch's)
Frozen apple juice (Lincoln or pure apple)
Colorless diet cream soda
Pure pineapple juice

SNACKS
Potato chips (no additives)
Rykrisp crackers and pure honey
Raisins (unsulfured)

MISCELLANEOUS
Pure honey
Pure maple syrup
Homemade vinegar and oil dressing
Sea salt
Pepper
Homemade soup

FORBIDDEN

CEREALS
Foods containing wheat flour (most cakes, cookies, bread, baked goods)
Corn
Cereal mixtures (Granola)

FRUITS
Fresh frozen or canned (Unless in own juice, without dyes)
Citrus (orange, lemon, lime, grapefruit)

VEGETABLES
Fresh frozen or canned
Corn
Mixed vegetables
Peas

MEATS
Luncheon meats, weiners
Bacon
Artificially colored hamburger or meat
Ham
Dyed salmon, lobster
Breaded meats
Meats with stuffing

BEVERAGES
Milk or any type of dairy drink with casein or whey
Fruit beverages except those so specified
Kool-Aid
Coffee Rich (yellow dye)
7 Up, Squirt, Teem, Cola, Dr. Pepper, Ginger ale

SNACKS
Corn chips — Fritos
Chocolate or anything with cocoa
Hard Candy
Ice Cream or sherbet

MISCELLANEOUS
Sugar
Bread, cake, cookies except on special recipes
Eggs
Dyed (colored) vitamins, pills, mouth wash, toothpaste, medicines,*
    cough syrups, etc.
Jelly or jam
Jell-O
Margarine or diet spreads (dyes or corn)
Peanut butter — peanuts
Sorbitol (corn)
Cheese

*Check with child's physician.

MULTIPLE FOOD ELMIMINATION DIET

Part 2

How Do You Do the Second Part of the Diet?

During Part 2 of the diet, one food is introduced into the diet, in excess, each day. Keep detailed records of how your child feels each day. Start with a teaspoon or 1/2 cup of the test food item and double the amount eaten every few hours, so that by the end of the day at least a normal amount has been ingested. Do any symptoms suddenly reappear? If there are no undesirable symptoms during the day, during the night or the next morning before breakfast, the food tested the day before is probably all right and may be eaten whenever desired. If the test food causes symptoms, stop eating it in all forms until you can secure the advice of your physician. Do not give your child another test food until the symptoms from the previous food test have subsided. Usually a parent will notice that symptoms are caused by a food within one hour. Rarely symptoms from a food are delayed for several hours. If Alka-Seltzer Antacid Formula without aspirin (gold foil) or Alka-Aid from the health food store, or the usual allergy medications are taken, your child's symptoms will often subside before the next test food is due to be added to the diet. If concerned, check with the doctor or nearest hospital.

REMEMBER: If one of the listed foods causes a reaction which is not helped by Alka-Seltzer in gold foil and which lasts for over 24 hours, DO NOT TRY to see the response to another possible problem food until the reaction has entirely subsided.

Watch closely to see what happens each day. One food might cause a stuffy nose, the next no reaction at all, the next a bellyache. Some reactions occur immediately, others in several hours. **If a food obviously causes severe symptoms, it should not be eaten.**

If you are uncertain if a food causes symptoms, discontinue it until the other foods have been checked. Then give your child the suspect food every five days, for example, on Tuesday and Saturday, and see if symptoms recur each time it is eaten.

NEVER TEST ANY FOOD WITHOUT YOUR DOCTOR'S ADVISE IF IT CAUSED SERIOUS MEDICAL PROBLEMS IN THE PAST. FOR EXAMPLE: IF EGG OR PEANUT CAUSED IMMEDIATE THROAT SWELLING OR FISH CAUSED SEVERE ASTHMA. IT IS UNSAFE TO TRY EVEN A SPECK OF THESE FOODS.

add	MILK	on	Day 8
add	WHEAT	on	Day 9
add	SUGAR	on	Day 10
add	EGG	on	Day 11
add	COCOA	on	Day 12
add	FOOD COLORING	on	Day 13
add	CORN	on	Day 14
add	PRESERVATIVES	on	Day 15
add	CITRUS	on	Day 16
add	PEANUT BUTTER	on	Day 17

Day 8 **The day you add milk,** give your child lots of milk, cottage cheese and whipped cream sweetened with pure maple syrup or honey. No butter, margarine or yellow cheese unless you are absolutely certain they contain NO yellow dyes.

Day 9 **The day you add wheat,** add plain soda crackers or wheat cereal. If your child had trouble from milk, be sure NOT to give milk products. Use Italian bread or kosher bread because these should not contain milk (casein or whey), but always read labels to be sure. You can bake if you like, but you must not use eggs or sugar. Remember, your child can eat no dairy products or drink any milk if he seemed worse in any way on the milk day. If milk caused no problem, milk products may be eaten.

Day 10 **The day you add sugar,** give your child sugar cubes to eat and add granulated sugar to the allowed foods. If milk or wheat caused trouble, they must be avoided or you can't tell if sugar is tolerated. Many children react within one hour after 4-8 sugar cubes.

Day 11 **The day you add egg,** give your child eggs in usual forms, cooked or as eggnog. Give custard. Remember, again, no wheat, milk or sugar can be consumed if any of these caused problems.

Day 12 **The day you add cocoa,** give your child dark chocolate and cocoa. Only if your child had no trouble with sugar and milk can you give milk chocolate. You can make hot chocolate with water, cocoa (pure Hershey's cocoa powder) and honey or pure maple syrup. No candy bars are allowed because most contain corn. Remember, no milk, wheat, sugar, dyes or eggs are allowed if any of these caused symptoms.

Day 13 **The day you add food coloring,** give your child Jell-O, jelly or artificially colored fruit beverages (soda pop, Kool-Aid), Popsicles or cereal. Try to give lots of yellow, purple and red items because your child might react to only one of these colors. Remember to avoid milk, wheat, Coca-Cola or sugar in all forms if any of these were a problem. If sugar caused symptoms, use honey, or pure maple syrup as a sweetener or buy dietetic pop and gelatin. If milk, wheat or sugar were tolerated, they may be eaten.

Day 14 **The day you add corn,** give your child corn, corn meal, corn flakes and popcorn. The latter can be made with salt and Crisco, if food coloring was a problem. If milk, wheat, sugar, dyes, eggs or chocolate cause trouble, you can't give them on the same day you give corn. If you do, and your child is worse, you won't be able to tell which is at fault. Do not use butter on popcorn if your child has a milk sensitivity.

Day 15 The day you add preservatives, give your child foods which contain any preservatives or food additives. Read every label. In particular, eat luncheon meat, bologna, hot dogs, bread or other baked goods, or soups which contain preservatives and additives.

Day 16 The day you add citrus, give your child a large amount of lemon, lime, grapefruit or orange as fresh fruit, or in juice and gelatin. Avoid artificial dyes if food colors were a problem. Avoid gelatin if sugar was a problem.

Day 17 The day you add peanut butter, give your child lots of peanut butter or peanuts. Test for this only if it's a favorite food. Use Rye-krisp if no wheat is allowed. Use pure peanut butter without additives (Smuckers).

SPECIAL TIPS FOR THE
MULTIPLE ELIMINATION DIET

The "allowed" foods can be selected, combined and eaten in any quantity.

For a beverage, you can mix the allowed fruits in the blender with spring water and honey or pure maple syrup.

Your child's usual medications can be taken during the diet. If your child improves, you may find the medicine is needed less often by the end of the first week. Try to use only white pills (crushed for small children and placed in applesauce or mashed potatoes) or colorless liquids. Most liquid medications contain corn, sugar and dyes which can cause symptoms in some children. Check with your physician about any questions you may have.

Once you determine which foods cause specific symptoms, you must discuss the problem with your physician. Some foods cannot be omitted for indefinite periods of time if a child's nutrition is to be maintained.

Do not try the diet when your child has an infection or is receiving an antibiotic.

Although the symptoms may vary, food sensitivities are often evident in several family members. One child might have headaches, another a stuffy nose, and a third, hyperactivity. The same food, e.g. milk, may be a problem for several generations of a family. For this reason, make cooking easier by placing the entire family on the diet. A fringe benefit may be that you may relieve some "emotional or learn-to-live-with-it" health problems caused by a certain food in several family members.

If your child has asthma, add the test food back into the diet with extreme care. It is possible that an unsuspected food could precipitate a sudden severe asthma attack. Have asthma medications on hand during Part 2 of the diet.

If your child refuses the diet, try offering a reward. Promise a gala party if there is no cheating and if it is obvious that the child is truly trying very hard to cooperate in every way. The party should take place AFTER both parts of the diet are completed. Give your child the foods which caused symptoms and this will be a double check confirming the effect of these foods on your child.

We sincerely hope this diet will help your child.

Additional details about this diet available in:

ALLERGIES AND THE HYPERACTIVE CHILD

ALLERGIES AND YOUR FAMILY

Practical Allergy Research Foundation
P.O. Box 60
Buffalo, NY 14223
716-875-5578

© Doris J. Rapp, M.D. 1989

THE RITALIN PROBLEM

Over 1 million children, 6 years or older, will take Ritalin by 1999. This drug is prescribed for the Attention Deficit Disorder (ADD) or for impulsive children who are easily distracted and cannot concentrate. Some, also, have hyperactivity. This drug is a class 2 narcotic.

Although many children are less active when they receive Ritalin, some lose weight, grow slowly because of poor appetite, have sleep problems, lose their personality and act like zombies. Parents often complain that when the drug wears off after school, their children act more uncontrollable than usual.

Less common side effects include agitation, nervousness, headaches, nausea, abdominal pain, a rapid heartbeat, dizziness, bed wetting, mood swings, tension, and anxiety. Infrequent complaints are blurred vision, joint pain, fever, hives and a tendency to seizures. Rarely it causes psychotic or suicidal behavior if the drug is not tapered slowly when it is being discontinued.

DO PARENTS HAVE OTHER CHOICES?

Yes. The Physician's Desk Reference (in drugstores or libraries) clearly states that Ritalin should never be prescribed if the problem is due to some environmental factor. Many children's symptoms are due to foods or pollen, molds, dust, and chemicals which are environmental. One answer, there-fore, is to find if the cause could be an allergy and to eliminate or treat it.

Another choice is to try Calm Kids. This is a natural gentle tranquilizer composed of amino acids, vitamins, and minerals which calm or quiet the brain. For more information write or call the Pain and Stress Center, 5282 Medical Drive, #160, San Antonio, TX 78229, 512-696-1674.

INDEX

— — — — — — — — — ORDER FORM — — — — — — — — —
(Please Print)

Name _____

Address _____

City_____ State _____ Zip _____

I would like to purchase:	Price	Quantity	Total
The Impossible Child	$10.95	_____	_____
Allergies and the Hyperactive Child	$ 9.95	_____	_____
Allergies and Your Family	$12.95	_____	_____

Merchandise Total _____

Shipping and Handling* + _____

Subtotal _____

New York State Residents Only - Sales Tax 8% + _____

TOTAL AMOUNT ENCLOSED _____

*1 book, $2.50, each additional book, $1.00
Allow 6 weeks for delivery. Foreign orders use U.S. funds.

We accept:

Visa Account Number: _____ Exp. Date_____

Master Card Number: _____ Exp. Date_____

*Signature:_____

NO CASH OR C.O.D. ORDERS

Mail check to:
Practical Allergy Research Foundation (PARF)
P.O. Box 60
Buffalo, N.Y. 14223-0060

☐ Send audio cassette information regarding diet, home, chemical avoidance and infants.

☐ Send video cassette information demonstrating typical responses to foods, chemicals, dust, molds, or pollen.

— — — — — — — — — **ORDER FORM** — — — — — — — — —

(Please Print)

Name _____

Address _____

City_____ State _____ Zip _____

I would like to purchase: **Price**   **Quantity**   **Total**

The Impossible Child $10.95   _____   _____

*Allergies and the
    Hyperactive Child* $ 9.95   _____   _____

Allergies and Your Family $12.95   _____   _____

Merchandise Total   _____

Shipping and Handling* +   _____

Subtotal   _____

New York State Residents Only - Sales Tax 8% +   _____

TOTAL AMOUNT ENCLOSED   _____

*1 book, $2.50, each additional book, $1.00
Allow 6 weeks for delivery. Foreign orders use U.S. funds.

We accept:

Visa Account Number: _____ Exp. Date_____

Master Card Number: _____ Exp. Date_____

*Signature:_____

NO CASH OR C.O.D. ORDERS

Mail check to:
Practical Allergy Research Foundation (PARF)
P.O. Box 60
Buffalo, N.Y. 14223-0060

☐ Send audio cassette information regarding diet, home, chemical
    avoidance and infants.

☐ Send video cassette information demonstrating typical responses
    to foods, chemicals, dust, molds, or pollen.

– – – – – – – – – **ORDER FORM** – – – – – – – – –
(Please Print)

Name _____

Address _____

City_____ State _____ Zip _____

I would like to purchase:	**Price**	**Quantity**	**Total**
The Impossible Child	$10.95	_____	_____
Allergies and the Hyperactive Child	$ 9.95	_____	_____
Allergies and Your Family	$12.95	_____	_____

Merchandise Total _____

Shipping and Handling* + _____

Subtotal _____

New York State Residents Only - Sales Tax 8% + _____

TOTAL AMOUNT ENCLOSED _____

*1 book, $2.50, each additional book, $1.00
Allow 6 weeks for delivery. Foreign orders use U.S. funds.

We accept:

Visa Account Number: _____ Exp. Date_____

Master Card Number: _____ Exp. Date_____

*Signature:_____

NO CASH OR C.O.D. ORDERS

Mail check to:
Practical Allergy Research Foundation (PARF)
P.O. Box 60
Buffalo, N.Y. 14223-0060

☐ Send audio cassette information regarding diet, home, chemical avoidance and infants.

☐ Send video cassette information demonstrating typical responses to foods, chemicals, dust, molds, or pollen.

Doris J. Rapp, M.D., F.A.A.A., F.A.A.P., is a Clinical
Assistant Professor of Pediatrics at the State University of
New York at Buffalo. She received her B.A. degree, magna cum
laude, and an M.A. degree from the University of Buffalo.
She obtained her medical degree from New York University.
She completed her pediatric internship and residency at
Buffalo Children's Hospital. An additional two year clinical
and research residency program was completed in allergy and
immunology. She practiced traditional allergy for 18 years. A
turning point in her life occurred during a medical conference
in 1975. At that time she first heard about some newer and
more precise methods to diagnose and treat a wide range of
illnesses due to foods and chemicals. With immense skepticism,
she tried the newer diagnostic and therapeutic methods
suggested by clinical ecologists, or specialists in environmental
medicine. She found that many patients' symptoms could be
produced and eliminated, at will, by using the newer more
precise variations of traditional allergy testing and treatment.
She could then help some patients, often without the need of
drugs, in a manner and to a degree which was not possible
before. She subsequently conducted medical research, published
medical articles, presented in medical conferences, wrote
books for the public, and prepared teaching video and audio
tapes. These have helped those who are interested to recognize
and understand more about the types of illness caused by
foods, odors, and common allergenic substances.